40 Hadith on Femininity: How to Be a Good Woman

By Nabeel Azeez

ISBN: 978-1-7349208-4-0

Claim Your Exclusive Bonuses

As a "thank you" for purchasing *40 Hadith on Femininity: How to Be a Good Woman*, we'd like to offer you the following bonuses, gratis.

1. A PDF copy of this book
2. A PDF of the "matn," containing only the verses of Quran, hadith of the Prophet ﷺ and statements of the Companions and Scholars on which this book is based

To claim your bonuses, simply email a copy of your receipt to hello@muslimman.com.

Extra credit: We'd also be grateful if you'd post a picture of yourself holding your copy of the book on social media and tag @beamuslimman.

Acknowledgements

Praise be to Allah who made us Muslims and honored us over many of His creations. May Allah's blessings and peace be on our beloved Prophet Muhammad, as many times as the mindful remember him and as many times as the heedless forget.

This book is dedicated to Quraisha Azeez. Ever since you became a mother, you dedicated your life to us. You raised three children on your own while Dad was away to provide for us. After Allah's Grace, it was you who made me the man I am today. You are an excellent mother. I am a terrible son. May Allah grant you Al-Firdaws Al-A'la.

Jazakumullahu khairan and thank you to Dr. Salah Sharief and the entire Wordsmiths team. You went above and beyond in researching, translating, and editing this book. It wouldn't exist without you. Readers should check out your website, wordsmiths.org.uk.

Thank you to Kristin McTiernan who got this book ready for publishing. You made my life easy. God bless you. Readers should check out your website, nonsensefreeeditor.com.

To non-Muslims who read this work, I invite you to convert to Islam and gain felicity in this life and the next.

Glory be to your Lord, the Lord of Might, beyond anything they describe. And peace be upon the Messengers. And praise be to Allah, the Lord of all the worlds.

– Nabeel Azeez, founder of MuslimMan™

Table of Contents

Introduction xi

Instead of Him, They Invoke Only Female Gods xi

Glory Be to Him Who Created All Things in Pairs xii

A Journey to True *Unūthah* xv

Works are Judged by Intentions xvii

1 | The Gracious Woman 1

1 Her Character and Manners are Impeccable 1

2 She is a Philanthropist 5

3 She is a Supporter 9

4 She is Creative 13

5 She is a Teacher 16

6 She Chooses Words Wisely 20

7 She Judges Not 26

8 She is Resilient 29

9 She is a Gracious Host 33

10 She is Courteous 36

2 | The Interdependent Woman 40

11 She Honours Her Parents 40

12 She is Light-Hearted 44

13 She Embodies Sisterhood 46

14 She is a Wife 51

15 She is Ever Loyal and Dutiful 55

16 She is Gentle 60

17 She is Financially Responsible 63

18 She is Motherly 67

19 She Cares 71
20 She is a Guardian 74
3 | The Self-Aware Woman 78
21 She is Feminine 78
22 She is Altruistic 81
23 She is Modest 85
24 She is Fit and Well 90
25 She Values Cleanliness and Self-Care 94
26 She has *Ghayrah* 98
27 She has *Ḥayā'* 102
28 She Knows Her Limits 107
29 She Hones Her Mind 111
30 She is Organised 115
4 | The Mindful Woman 118
31 Her Faith is in Allah Alone 118
32 She Intends Good 123
33 She is Consistent in her Worship 127
34 She Reflects 132
35 She Remembers Allah 135
36 She has *Taqwā* 139
37 She Practises *Tawakkul* 144
38 She is Grateful 149
39 She Repents 153
40 She is Prepared for Death 157
5 | A Final Word 161

بِسۡمِ ٱللَّهِ ٱلرَّحۡمَٰنِ ٱلرَّحِيمِ

الحمد لله ربّ العالمين، الرّحمن الرّحيم، الذي خلقنا مِن نفس واحدة وخلق منها زوجها وبثّ منهما رجالاً كثيرًا ونساء، والصلاة والسّلام على سيّد الأنبياء وخاتم الأنبياء، سيّدنا محمد المصطفى، وعلى أمهات المؤمنين والمؤمنات، وآله الطاهرين والطاهرات، وصحابته أجمعين، ومَن تبعهم بإحسان إلى يوم الدين. وبعد:

All praise is for Allah, the Lord of the Worlds. The Very-Merciful, the All-Merciful, Who created us from a single soul. From it He created its mate, and through them both spread forth many men and women. May blessings and salutations be upon the Master of the Prophets and the Seal of the Prophets, our master Muhammad al-Muṣṭafā; upon the mothers of the believing men and women; upon his pure family, both male and female; upon all of his Ṣaḥābah; and upon all who follow them in goodness until the Day of Requital.

INTRODUCTION

Instead of Him, They Invoke Only Female Gods

There is an ancient enemy, as old as the days of Eden, bent upon mankind's destruction. Unseen, he waits at every hill and hollow. The well of our thoughts is poisoned by foul whispers that sound fair and sweet; our gaze is made a flight of arrows to wound our very souls; our tongues are set loose like wild animals, lashing out against their owners and others alike. The enemy is the Shayṭān. His goal is our eternal damnation.

Allah, in His infinite Mercy, has laid bare the enemy's machinations. The strategies and tactics he will use against us have been made crystal clear:

إِن يَدْعُونَ مِن دُونِهِۦٓ إِلَّآ إِنَـٰثًا وَإِن يَدْعُونَ إِلَّا شَيْطَـٰنًا مَّرِيدًا (١١٧) لَّعَنَهُ ٱللَّهُ ۘ
وَقَالَ لَأَتَّخِذَنَّ مِنْ عِبَادِكَ نَصِيبًا مَّفْرُوضًا (١١٨) وَلَأُضِلَّنَّهُمْ وَلَأُمَنِّيَنَّهُمْ وَلَـَٔامُرَنَّهُمْ
فَلَيُبَتِّكُنَّ ءَاذَانَ ٱلْأَنْعَـٰمِ وَلَـَٔامُرَنَّهُمْ فَلَيُغَيِّرُنَّ خَلْقَ ٱللَّهِ ۚ وَمَن يَتَّخِذِ ٱلشَّيْطَـٰنَ وَلِيًّا مِّن دُونِ
ٱللَّهِ فَقَدْ خَسِرَ خُسْرَانًا مُّبِينًا (١١٩)

"Instead of Him, they invoke only female gods; and they invoke none but Satan, the rebel - cursed by Allah - who said, 'I will surely take from Your servants an appointed share. I will mislead them; I will delude them with vain hopes; I will command them, whereby they shall slit the ears of cattle; and I will command them, whereby they shall alter

Allah's creation!' Whoever takes Satan as a patron instead of Allah incurs a manifest loss."[1]

The pagans of Arabia carved idols in feminine form; the modern world has made the feminine form an idol. We are told to 'celebrate' it. The word in its original sense means the public performance of a religious rite. The celebration of this form means to unclothe and flaunt it, to parody it through dress up (transvestitism), make-believe (transgenderism), or to reduce it to merely a man with missing parts (feminism). Each and every case is an attempt to denigrate and disfigure Allah's creation. It is the enemy's plan coming to fruition.

There is a reason feminism comes in waves like the invading forces of an alien armada. It is an idea wholly alien to our fiṭrah, an attack on that most basic postulate of reason: that men and women are not the same. Yet, with each wave, ground is given and the inexorable march to androgyny continues.

Glory Be to Him Who Created All Things in Pairs

سُبْحَـٰنَ ٱلَّذِى خَلَقَ ٱلْأَزْوَٰجَ كُلَّهَا مِمَّا تُنۢبِتُ ٱلْأَرْضُ وَمِنْ أَنفُسِهِمْ وَمِمَّا لَا يَعْلَمُونَ

"Glory be to Him Who created all things in pairs, of whatever the earth grows, and of humans themselves, and of that which they do not know."[2]

The word *azwāj* is the plural form of *zawj*, which means two things of the same kind or a match of the other. The *āyah* indicates that this pairing is the natural state across the animal and botanical kingdoms. Every child, fruit, and flower can only ever be born through procreation of these pairs. The *mufassirūn*, who are the commentators of the Qur'an, often refer to *azwāj* as kinds and categories. This is

---

[1] Qur'an, 4:117-119.
[2] Qur'an, 36:36.

because the term is also used to indicate contrast, such as that of cold and heat, land and water, sorrow and happiness, health and sickness, all of which are referred to as *azwāj*. Within each of these are a myriad of degrees and differences and kinds, as no two pairs are alike.

As a pair, Islam has divided the roles of men and women, and has made them complementing halves of a greater whole. A symbiont circle, a perfect *Yin* and *Yang*–the masculine and the feminine. The following hadith points to this fact:

إِنَّ النِّسَاءَ شَقَائِقُ الرِّجَالِ

"Women are men's counterparts."[3]

Allah states in the Qur'an that "Men are women's caretakers, as Allah has provisioned them over women, and because of the wealth they have spent."[4] In Islam, man bears the burden of provision and security and of upholding familial and communal honour. He is encouraged to actively work to source a halal income to fend for and support his family. He is encouraged to pray in congregation and take part in public roles and discourse. Conversely, the role of the woman is maintaining the household. She is the consoler, comforter, and counsel of her husband, and she forms the foundation of the family structure through teaching the next generation morality, ethics, mercy, and appreciation.

A careful examination of the Sharia reveals that one of its aims is to reduce a woman's financial and public roles. Hence, we see that her financial testimony and inheritance are both half that of a man's. We see that she is due a dowry and financial upkeep. We see that she cannot travel without a male relative or some legal substitute, and her prayer at home carries greater virtue than her praying in a mosque. All

---

[3] Abū Dāwūd al-Sijistānī, *Sunan Abī Dāwūd*, 236; Muḥammad ibn ʿĪsā al-Tirmidhī, *Jāmiʿ al-Tirmidhī*, 113; Abū Muhammad al-Dārimī, *Sunan al-Dārimī*, 759.
[4] Qur'an, 4:34.

of this is so she may focus on the most vital of all tasks: ensuring the moral and spiritual upkeep of her household.

For feminism, this is simply not enough. Feminism opposes femininity and wants women to do away with their innate feminine qualities, because it ultimately values masculine traits and masculine roles. The female idol of the modern West was fashioned by the groping hands of immoral men. It wants women to be career-driven public figures, dominating high earners, and even encourages female promiscuity. The new woman is a doppelganger of the very patriarchy they claim is evil and oppressive. Human worth, it seems, has been reduced to earning potential and public influence.

Earning money and doing business are impermissible for women, but that is not their natural role and the Sharia sets far greater aims and objectives for them. It is only our deep love of, and attachment to, this material world that causes us to view and measure everything through a materialistic lens.

Islamic manliness (*futūwwah*) and womanliness (*unūthah*) are not diametrically opposed. Men and women are not mortal enemies locked in an eternal struggle, despite what certain strains of feminism would have us believe. Yet, neither are they interchangeable. Islam has allocated each a clear role, rights, and responsibilities oriented towards the flourishing and preservation of the self, the family, and then society.

وَلَيْسَ ٱلذَّكَرُ كَٱلْأُنثَىٰ ۖ

"...and the male is not like the female."[5]

---

[5] Qur'an, 3:36.

A Journey to True *Unūthah*

This book has been written as a counterpart, a *zawj* one might say, of the *arbaʿīn* (40 hadith collection) on *futūwwah* entitled, *40 Hadith on Masculinity: How to Be a Good Man.* The first book was aimed at Muslim men, serving as a primer from which they could begin their journey to true masculinity: Islamic *futūwwah,* pure and uninfluenced by modern subservience to feminism or the male knee-jerk reactions to the same. That book also served as a guide for a woman to understand the standard by which the men in her life should be measured against, so she can support them in becoming better Muslim men; she can look for the correct qualities when accepting or rejecting a potential match.

The text in front of you seeks to do much the same. However, here the focus has now shifted to Islamic femininity. It is hoped that an arbaʿīn such as this will help refocus and reset the women that make up the backbone of Islamic society and help them to reject the influence of Shayṭān, returning to the Sunnah of our beloved Prophet ﷺ and that of his noble wives رضي الله عنهن and Ṣaḥābah رضي الله عنهم. Its second objective is to provide male readers with a benchmark for what is expected of a good Muslim woman and to help guide them in finding a wife with the correct mindset and qualities.

The *arbaʿīn* structure has been selected for the following reasons: (i) to ensure that the book remains focused on the goal of codifying *unūthah,* as restrictions ensure that words are not wasted and limit digression; (ii) to keep the text itself succinct and easily digestible, as the book is intended as a primer to give readers a brief overview of the subject; and (iii) to match the counterpart collection *40 Hadith on Masculinity: How to Be a Good Man.*

The book is divided into four sections, each comprising ten core hadiths, covering qualities established from the *fiṭrah,* that are further explained with commentary, Quranic verses, and additional hadiths. The first book began by focusing on the internal qualities a man must develop to become closer to Allah, before extending outward to his personal qualities, familial qualities and duties, and ultimately his outward interpersonal qualities. The structure was one of outward growth, as the duties of man take him outside to face the world. This book is the reverse of its counterpart.

It begins with a woman's relationship with the wider world, her duties towards neighbours and guests, and her imperative role in Islamic society. The second section then moves inward, focusing on her relationship with her family and her duties therein, looking at all the roles she plays in the functioning of a healthy family structure and highlighting the noble status of that most prized and beloved position: motherhood. The third section delves deeper still, covering her relationship with her own self and what she seeks to be; topics covered include femininity, self-care, self-value, and modesty. Finally, the last section represents the innermost sanctum of her soul and the most important relationship of all: her relationship with her Creator.

The core hadiths have been chosen by limiting the selection to only those hadiths that either: (i) are sayings of the Prophet ﷺ that address women; (ii) have been narrated by women; or (iii) are quotations of the Ṣaḥābiyāt رضي الله عنهن. Wherever possible, supporting hadiths have also followed the same methodology. Many qualities listed in this book are universal but apply differently to men and women; thus, sometimes hadiths have been brought that do not follow the above methodology.

It should be understood from the outset that this is not intended as a book on rights but a book on duties. Rights are what others owe to us; duties are what we owe to others. Despite what the world around us keeps telling us, despite the enemy's constant vile whisperings, we are not all bosses and gangsters, nor alphas and sigmas. We are not all kings and queens. We are slaves of Allah, owning neither the material things we care so much for, nor our own bodies themselves. We have been placed on Earth for a purpose and that is to worship Allah Alone. The fulfilment of our duties is the method in which we do so, and *in shā Allāh* will be the means for our ultimate salvation and a great reward.

The enemy attacks us systematically, overtly and covertly, and from all sides. It is time that we learned to defend ourselves.

وَإِنِّىٓ أُعِيذُهَا بِكَ وَذُرِّيَّتَهَا مِنَ ٱلشَّيْطَٰنِ ٱلرَّجِيمِ

"...and I seek Your protection for her and her offspring from Satan, the accursed."[6]

Works are Judged by Intentions

عَنْ أَمِيرِ الْمُؤْمِنِينَ أَبِي حَفْصٍ عُمَرَ بْنِ الْخَطَّابِ رَضِيَ اللهُ عَنْهُ قَالَ: سَمِعْتُ رَسُولَ اللهِ ﷺ يَقُولُ:

إِنَّمَا الْأَعْمَالُ بِالنِّيَّاتِ، وَإِنَّمَا لِكُلِّ امْرِئٍ مَا نَوَى، فَمَنْ كَانَتْ هِجْرَتُهُ إِلَى اللهِ وَرَسُولِهِ فَهِجْرَتُهُ إِلَى اللهِ وَرَسُولِهِ، وَمَنْ كَانَتْ هِجْرَتُهُ لِدُنْيَا يُصِيبُهَا أَوِ امْرَأَةٍ يَنْكِحُهَا فَهِجْرَتُهُ إِلَى مَا هَاجَرَ إِلَيْهِ.

Amīr al-Mu'minīn Sayyidunā Abū Ḥafṣ ʿUmar ibn al-Khaṭṭāb ﷺ *said:*

"I heard Allah's Messenger ﷺ *saying, 'Works are (judged) only by intentions, and so for everyone is only that which they intended. Thus, whosoever migrates to Allah and His Messenger, then his migration is to Allah and His Messenger; and whosoever migrates for some worldly thing he may acquire, or for a woman that he shall marry, then his migration is to that for which he migrated.'"*[7]

Just as each *sūrah* of the Qur'an has a name, so too do certain hadiths. This particular hadith is known as 'The Vanguard of Hadith

---

[6] Qur'an, 3:36.

[7] Aḥmad ibn Ḥanbal, *Musnad al-Imām Aḥmad*, 168; Muhammad ibn Ismāʿīl al-Bukhārī, *Ṣaḥīḥ al-Bukhārī*, 1, 54, 6689, 6953; Muslim ibn al-Ḥajjāj al-Naysābūrī, *Ṣaḥīḥ Muslim*, 1907a.

Collections' (*Ṭalīʿah Kutub al-Ḥadīth*).[8] ʿAbd al-Raḥmān ibn Mahdī states, "Whoever intends to author a book should start it with this hadith to alert the student of knowledge towards correcting his intention."[9]

Thus, it is our humble request that as we correct our intentions before beginning the task of compiling this collection, so too should you correct your own. May Allah accept this work from us, and may He make it a means of guidance for us all. *Āmīn.*

---

[8] Yūnus Jownpūrī, *Anwār al-Mishkāt*, vol. 1, p. 109.

[9] Ibn Daqīq al-ʿĪd, *Sharḥ al-Arbaʿīn*, p. 9.

1 | THE GRACIOUS WOMAN

1
Her Character and Manners are Impeccable

عَنْ عَائِشَةَ رَضِيَ اللَّهُ عَنْهَا قَالَتْ:

مَا كَانَ أَحْسَنُ خُلُقًا مِنْ رَسُولِ اللَّهِ صَلَّى اللهُ عَلَيْهِ وَسَلَّمَ مَا دَعَاهُ أَحَدٌ مِنْ أَصْحَابِهِ وَلَا مِنْ أَهْلِهِ إِلَّا قَالَ لَبَّيْكَ وَلِذَلِكَ أَنْزَلَ اللَّهُ عَزَّ وَجَلَّ:

وَإِنَّكَ لَعَلَى خُلُقٍ عَظِيمٍ[10]

Umm al-Mu'minīn Sayyidah ʿĀ'ishah ﵂ said:

"No one had better character than Allah's Messenger ﷺ. Neither his Ṣaḥābah nor his family called upon him except that he replied, 'I am at your service.' For this reason, Allah the Mighty and Majestic revealed the verse:

'And you are truly a man of outstanding character.'"[11]

Good character and good manners are essential qualities for any Muslim. A Muslim's manners must be impeccable. Umm al-Mu'minīn Sayyidah ʿĀ'ishah ﵂ spent her youth in the company of the most noble of all men ﷺ and recognised his character for what it was. When one's

[10] Qur'an, 68:4.
[11] Abū Bakr Aḥmad ibn al-Ḥusayn al-Bayhaqī, *Dalā'il al-Nubuwwah*, 119.

father is Sayyidunā Abū Bakr al-Ṣiddīq ﵁ and one's husband is Allah's Messenger ﷺ, how can one's own character not also be exemplary in every way? Good manners, etiquette, and unblemished character are not exclusively masculine qualities. In fact, they are the cornerstones of femininity. A woman is the nurturer, supporter, and affirmer in her family and for society as a whole. How she comports herself does not merely reflect on her, but serves as a reflection of the society she lives within. Umm al-Mu'minīn Sayyidah Zaynab bint Jaḥsh ﵂ narrates:

النَّبِيَّ صَلَّى اللَّهُ عَلَيْهِ وَسَلَّمَ دَخَلَ عَلَيْهَا فَزِعًا، يَقُولُ: لَا إِلَهَ إِلَّا اللَّهُ، وَيْلٌ لِلْعَرَبِ مِنْ شَرٍّ قَدْ اقْتَرَبَ، فُتِحَ الْيَوْمَ مِنْ رَدْمِ يَأْجُوجَ وَمَأْجُوجَ مِثْلُ هَذِهِ، وَحَلَّقَ بِإِصْبَعِهِ الْإِبْهَامِ وَالَّتِي تَلِيهَا، قَالَتْ زَيْنَبُ بِنْتُ جَحْشٍ، فَقُلْتُ: يَا رَسُولَ اللَّهِ، أَنَهْلِكُ وَفِينَا الصَّالِحُونَ؟ قَالَ: نَعَمْ، إِذَا كَثُرَ الْخَبَثُ.

The Prophet □ came to her (Zaynab) in a state of worry and said, "There is no God but Allah! Woe to the Arabs from an evil drawing near! An opening has been made today in the barrier of Gog and Magog like this," and he made a circle with his thumb and finger. Zaynab bint Jaḥsh said, "O Allah's Messenger, will we perish while there are righteous people among us?" The Prophet ﷺ said, "Yes, if wickedness prevails."[12]

A woman's behaviour shapes the people around her just as a man's does, but in a different way. A woman's manners and adherence to social etiquette are imprinted upon her children. Moreover, when women's manners and behaviours are allowed to become wicked in a given society, it collapses and we are left with a broken society, destroyed by the ravages of lewdness and shamelessness. One need only look to the ill effects of the multiple waves of rampant feminism in western societies to see where a lack of good manners and behaviours leads. So what then should a woman do? How should one

---

[12] *Ṣaḥīḥ al-Bukhārī*, 3168; *Ṣaḥīḥ Muslim*, 2880.

behave? Umm al-Mu'minīn Sayyidah ʿĀ'ishah narrates that Allah's Messenger ﷺ said,

$$\text{إِنَّ مِنْ أَكْمَلِ الْمُؤْمِنِينَ إِيمَانًا أَحْسَنُهُمْ خُلُقًا وَأَلْطَفُهُمْ بِأَهْلِهِ}$$

"Indeed the most complete believers in faith are those with the best character, and those who are kindest to their families."[13]

Imam Rashīd Aḥmad al-Gangohī ؒ explains that the definition of good character is to deal with the Creator and His creation in a manner that pleases the Creator.[14] Thus, we must show kindness to those we can influence, meaning all those who are in contact with us. This includes good conduct with one's sisters in wider society, by showing mutual respect and courtesy to other women. However, above all else, as the second half of the hadith emphasises, it is correct Islamic behaviour and principles within the home that exemplify good character. This is where a woman shapes the men and women of tomorrow and has the greatest influence on the men and women of today.

It is a sad state of affairs that sisters have been convinced by the 'woke mob' that good behaviour and *taqwā* are not desirable qualities; that a woman should be equal and not equitable to her male counterparts; that to have value you must become a 'girl boss', and all but become a man with differing sexual organs; and that a woman who fulfils her traditional role as a homemaker, supporter, and nurturer is somehow lesser and must be looked down upon. Muslim women should not be lured in by these depressing and trans-humanist ideas and should instead look to what Allah and His Messenger ﷺ have said is of merit and worthwhile. Umm al-Mu'minīn Sayyidah ʿĀ'ishah ؓ reported that Allah's Messenger ﷺ said,

$$\text{إِنَّ الْمُؤْمِنَ لَيُدْرِكُ بِحُسْنِ خُلُقِهِ دَرَجَةَ الصَّائِمِ الْقَائِمِ}$$

---

[13] *Jāmiʿ al-Tirmidhī*, 2612.
[14] Rashīd Aḥmad al-Gangohī, *al-Kawkab al-Durrī ʿalā Jāmiʿ al-Tirmidhī*, vol. 3, p. 590.

"Indeed by his good character the believer may reach the rank of one who regularly fasts and stands in nightly prayer."[15]

A woman does not need to be exactly as a man is to have worth, nor does she need to do exactly as a man does to earn respect and high reward; she need only be *good.* Whatever reward the men of her household gain through striving beyond the four walls of her house, she can gain by striving within those very walls.

---

[15] *Sunan Abī Dāwūd,* 4798.

2
She is a Philanthropist

عَنْ عَائِشَةَ:

أَنَّ بَعْضَ أَزْوَاجِ النَّبِيِّ صَلَّى اللهُ عَلَيْهِ وَسَلَّمَ قُلْنَ لِلنَّبِيِّ صَلَّى اللهُ عَلَيْهِ وَسَلَّمَ أَيُّنَا أَسْرَعُ بِكَ لُحُوقًا؟ قَالَ أَطْوَلُكُنَّ يَدًا. فَأَخَذُوا قَصَبَةً يَذْرَعُونَهَا فَكَانَتْ سَوْدَةُ أَطْوَلَهُنَّ يَدًا فَمَاتَتْ زَيْنَبُ أَوَّلَهُنَّ. فَعَلِمْنَا بَعْدُ أَنَّمَا كَانَتْ طُولَ يَدِهَا الصَّدَقَةُ وَكَانَتْ أَسْرَعَنَا لُحُوقًا بِهِ وَكَانَتْ تُحِبُّ الصَّدَقَةَ.

'Ā'ishah ؓ narrated:

"Some of the wives of the Prophet ﷺ asked him, 'Which of us will be the quickest to meet you after death?' The Prophet ﷺ said, 'The one with the longest hand.' They measured their hands with sticks and Sawdah had the longest hands amongst them, yet Zaynab was the first of them to die. It was then that we knew that the 'length of her hand' meant 'her charity'. She was the quickest to meet him and she loved to give charity."[16]

The generosity and charitableness of Umm al-Mu'minīn Sayyidah Zaynab ؓ was legendary. It was because of this notable quality that she was given distinction by the Prophet ﷺ in the above hadith. Imam Ḥākim ؓ explains in his *al-Mustadrak* that she was skilled with her hands and would tan and embroider hides, then give charity from her earnings for the sake of Allah.[17] What greater reward could she have earned than being the first of the wives of the Prophet ﷺ to join him in the next life?

It is no great secret that of all the creeds of the world, those who profess submission to Allah Alone have the 'longest hands'. We have developed a reputation for charitableness that even our staunchest enemies must begrudgingly accept. It is a well-documented fact and

---

[16] *Ṣaḥīḥ al-Bukhārī*, 1420; *Ṣaḥīḥ Muslim*, 2452.
[17] Taqī al-'Uthmānī, *Takmilah Fatḥ al-Mulhim*, vol. 5, p. 96.

wider society recognises this. But even amongst the most charitable people on the planet, it is perhaps equally well-known that our sisters give the most in charity. Women, who have been created to care for others, to be empathetic and loving and kind, should not be any other way. When a righteous sister sees another in pain and suffering, it is not in her nature to turn away, uncaring of her fellow human being's plight. If she can act, she *must* act; if she cannot, she nevertheless finds a way. Sayyidah Umm Bujayd ؓ narrates that she said:

قَالَتْ يَا رَسُولَ اللَّهِ إِنَّ الْمِسْكِينَ لَيَقُومُ عَلَى بَابِي فَمَا أَجِدُ لَهُ شَيْئًا أُعْطِيهِ إِيَّاهُ.

فَقَالَ لَهَا رَسُولُ اللَّهِ صَلَّى اللَّهُ عَلَيْهِ وَسَلَّمَ إِنْ لَمْ تَجِدِي شَيْئًا تُعْطِينَهُ إِيَّاهُ إِلَّا ظِلْفًا مُحْرَقًا فَادْفَعِيهِ إِلَيْهِ فِي يَدِهِ.

"O Allah's Messenger, the poor come to my door, but I cannot find anything to give them."

Allah's Messenger ﷺ replied, "Even if you can find nothing but a burnt trotter, place it in their hand."[18]

This is how the charity of a Muslim should be. If one is asked for help, it must be given. Even if it means searching your house for something, *anything*, to give. The asker should never leave empty handed; the giver should never say no. It was the practice of the Prophet ﷺ to always give when asked. When he was unable to do so, he would say that he did not have anything to give, rather than saying no. Any small thing that we give in charity is replaced with a mountain of reward. Umm al-Mu'minīn Sayyidah ʿĀ'ishah ؓ reported that Allah's Messenger ﷺ said:

إِنَّ اللَّهَ لَيُرَبِّي لِأَحَدِكُمُ التَّمْرَةَ وَاللُّقْمَةَ كَمَا يُرَبِّي أَحَدُكُمْ فَلُوَّهُ أَوْ فَصِيلَهُ حَتَّى يَكُونَ مِثْلَ أُحُدٍ

[18] *Jāmiʿ al-Tirmidhī*, 665.

"Indeed Allah will raise up a date or a morsel given in charity, just as one of you raises his colt or young camel, until it becomes like Mount Uḥud."[19]

This highly profitable exchange alone should be enough for a Muslim to strive to give more in charity and emulate the Mothers of the Believers and the Ṣaḥābiyāt ﵅ in their giving. Allah not only grants the Muslim far more in exchange, but He also grants such a philanthropist safety from the Hellfire. Umm al-Mu'minīn Sayyidah ʿĀ'ishah ﵂ also reported that Allah's Messenger ﷺ said to her:

يَا عَائِشَةُ، اسْتَتِرِي مِنَ النَّارِ وَلَوْ بِشِقِّ تَمْرَةٍ؛ فَإِنَّهَا تَسُدُّ مِنَ الْجَائِعِ مَسَدَّهَا مِنَ الشَّبْعَانِ.

"ʿĀ'ishah, protect yourself from the Fire, even with half a date's charity, for it will serve to placate the hungry somewhat the way it placates the satiated."[20]

From this we can see the value in giving aid to those in need, regardless of how small a gesture it is. Allah has made women's natural disposition one of empathy, and thus made it easier for them to reap the rewards of investing their goodwill and kindness in the hearts of the needy. What we ourselves consume is processed within our bodies and gone within a matter of days; what we give out in aid to others is stored away in the vaults of eternity, to be repaid manifold by Allah in the Hereafter.

عَنْ عَائِشَةَ، أَنَّهُمْ ذَبَحُوا شَاةً وَأَنَّهُم تَصَدَّقُوا بِهَا، فَقَالَ النَّبِيُّ صَلَّى اللهُ عَلَيْهِ وَسَلَّمَ: مَا بَقِيَ مِنْهَا؟ قَالَتْ: مَا بَقِيَ مِنْهَا إِلَّا كَتِفُهَا. قَالَ: بَقِيَ كُلُّهَا غَيْرَ كَتِفِهَا.

Umm al-Mu'minīn Sayyidah ʿĀ'ishah ﵂ reported that they slaughtered a sheep and gave charity from it. The Prophet ﷺ asked her, "What remains of it?" Umm al-Mu'minīn Sayyidah ʿĀ'ishah ﵂

[19] Muḥammad ibn Hibbān al-Bustī, *Ṣaḥīḥ Ibn Ḥibbān*, 3317.
[20] Aḥmad ibn Ḥanbal, *Musnad al-Imām Aḥmad*, 24501.

replied, "Nothing remains except its shoulder." The Prophet ﷺ said, "All remains except its shoulder."[21]

The only way to truly benefit from this material world is to give it away. Women, being naturally more giving, are granted even greater opportunities than their male counterparts to meaningfully benefit themselves and their loved ones in the Hereafter. Umm al-Mu'minīn Sayyidah ʿĀ'ishah ﵂ reported that Allah's Messenger ﷺ said,

إِذَا تَصَدَّقَتِ الْمَرْأَةُ مِنْ طَعَامِ زَوْجِهَا غَيْرَ مُفْسِدَةٍ كَانَ لَهَا أَجْرُهَا، وَلِزَوْجِهَا بِمَا كَسَبَ، وَلِلْخَازِنِ مِثْلُ ذَلِكَ

"When a woman gives charity from her husband's provision without wasting his property, she will be rewarded for it. Her husband too will receive reward for what he earned, and the storekeeper will also gain the like thereof."[22]

The reward is not diminished by her giving from her husband's earned wealth in charity. It is in fact multiplied. She gains reward for it, her husband gains reward for it, and anyone involved in the matter also gains reward for it, without anyone's reward being diminished. Islam is the religion of the charitable. There is a caveat to this, however, in that the scholars state that it should be spent in a manner that does not cause loss or financial harm to her husband, or that it should be spent on the family of her husband in things that are conducive to good.[23]

---

[21] *Jāmiʿ al-Tirmidhī*, 2470.
[22] *Ṣaḥīḥ al-Bukhārī*, 1437.
[23] Ibn Ḥajar al-ʿAsqalānī, *Fatḥ al-Bārī bi-Sharḥ Ṣaḥīḥ al-Bukhārī*, vol. 5, p. 89.

3
She is a Supporter

عَنْ سَهْلِ بْنِ سَعْدٍ السَّاعِدِيِّ، قَالَ:

لَمَّا كُسِرَتْ عَلَى رَأْسِ رَسُولِ اللَّهِ صلى الله عليه وسلم الْبَيْضَةُ، وَأُدْمِيَ وَجْهُهُ، وَكُسِرَتْ رَبَاعِيَتُهُ، وَكَانَ عَلِيٌّ يَخْتَلِفُ بِالْمَاءِ فِي الْمِجَنِّ، وَجَاءَتْ فَاطِمَةُ تَغْسِلُ عَنْ وَجْهِهِ الدَّمَ، فَلَمَّا رَأَتْ فَاطِمَةُ ـ عَلَيْهَا السَّلاَمُ ـ الدَّمَ يَزِيدُ عَلَى الْمَاءِ كَثْرَةً عَمَدَتْ إِلَى حَصِيرٍ فَأَحْرَقَتْهَا وَأَلْصَقَتْهَا عَلَى جُرْحِ رَسُولِ اللَّهِ صلى الله عليه وسلم فَرَقَأَ الدَّمُ.

Sahl ibn Saʿd al-Sāʿidī narrates:

When the helmet broke on the head of Allah's Messenger ﷺ and his face was covered with blood, and his incisor tooth was broken, ʿAlī brought water in his shield, while Fāṭimah washed the blood from his face. When Fāṭimah noticed that the bleeding increased due to the water, she took a mat of woven palm leaves, burnt it, and placed it on the wound of Allah's Messenger ﷺ, whereupon the bleeding stopped.[24]

Islam has not made a woman's role or position any less than a man's. As human beings, we are all equal in the Sight of Allah and will be judged according to our own merits. A man will not be given preferential treatment on the Day of Requital due to his gender, nor will a woman be afforded leniency on account of hers. The roles of men and women, however, are very different.

Whereas men are required to earn a living and put food on the table, women are required to care for the children in the household and to look after themselves, their homes, and the property therein. Whereas men are required to stand on the field of battle when called upon to do so, women are not. This does not make them *less*, as the western feminist movement would have you believe. Their roles are simply *different*. In the above hadith we see this difference on display.

---

[24] *Ṣaḥīḥ al-Bukhārī*, 5722.

The Prophet ﷺ was fighting on the battlefield on the Day of Uḥud. His daughter, Sayyidah Fāṭimah ‎رضي الله عنها‎, was present at Uḥud too but she was not fighting. She was not expected to do so. Yet, her actions were no less heroic on the day, and we can see from this that the role of the supporter is every bit as important as the role of a man. Indeed, mastery of the skills required to carry out such roles is commendable and worthy of praise and reward.

Further examples of this can be seen from other noble women on that very same field of battle. Sayyidunā Anas ‎رضي الله عنه‎ narrates:

لَمَّا كَانَ يَوْمُ أُحُدٍ انْهَزَمَ النَّاسُ عَنِ النَّبِيِّ صلى الله عليه وسلم، قَالَ: وَلَقَدْ رَأَيْتُ عَائِشَةَ بِنْتَ أَبِي بَكْرٍ وَأُمَّ سُلَيْمٍ وَإِنَّهُمَا لَمُشَمِّرَتَانِ، أَرَى خَدَمَ سُوقِهِمَا، تَنْقُزَانِ الْقِرَبَ – وَقَالَ غَيْرُهُ تَنْقُلاَنِ الْقِرَبَ – عَلَى مُتُونِهِمَا، ثُمَّ تُفْرِغَانِهِ فِي أَفْوَاهِ الْقَوْمِ، ثُمَّ تَرْجِعَانِ فَتَمْلآنِهَا، ثُمَّ تَجِيئَانِ فَتُفْرِغَانِهَا فِي أَفْوَاهِ الْقَوْمِ.

"On the Day of Uḥud when people retreated and left the Prophet ﷺ, I saw 'Ā'ishah bint Abū Bakr and Umm Sulaym, with their robes tucked so that their ankle-bangles were visible,[25] hurrying with water skins (in another narration, 'carrying the water skins on their backs'). They would pour water into the mouths of people, then return to refill the water skins, before coming back again to pour water into the mouths of the people once again."[26]

A similar narration is given with regard to Sayyidah Umm Salīṭ ‎رضي الله عنها‎.[27]

These hadiths highlight two key points in relation to our discussion. Firstly, the women amongst the Ṣaḥābah ‎رضي الله عنهم‎ were every bit as brave as their male counterparts, though their bravery was exhibited in entirely different ways – they served the army in supporting roles. Often, so-called 'feminist Muslimahs' will try to use such examples to portray Islam in a 'woke' modernist light, whereas in reality the narrations

[25] Uḥud occurred before the requirement of hijab, and this was the field of war. This should not be used as an excuse for sisters to show the lower portions of their legs to adhere to the poor 'social norms' of western society.

[26] *Ṣaḥīḥ al-Bukhārī*, 2880.

[27] *Ṣaḥīḥ al-Bukhārī*, 2881.

clearly show that the womenfolk were not present on the field as fighters, but to support the men in what they had to do, and they were duly commended for these actions.[28] Secondly, we see that they were exceptionally good at what they did in these supporting roles. Whether serving water, providing medical aid to weary and injured soldiers, or carrying out their day-to-day tasks in their homes, they did their jobs efficiently and well, seeking only to please Allah, thus earning rewards equal to those of the warriors, *zakāh*-payers, and frequenters of the *masjid.*

During a conversation with Sayyidunā Ibn Aʿbud ﷺ, Sayyidunā ʿAlī ﷺ explained how his wife, the beloved daughter of the Prophet ﷺ, would work hard at home, stating,

إِنَّهَا جَرَّتْ بِالرَّحَى حَتَّى أَثَّرَ فِي يَدِهَا وَاسْتَقَتْ بِالْقِرْبَةِ حَتَّى أَثَّرَ فِي نَحْرِهَا وَكَنَسَتِ الْبَيْتَ حَتَّى اغْبَرَّتْ ثِيَابُهَا

"She turned the millstone by hand until it calloused her hand, she carried the waterskin until it marked the upper portion of her chest, and she swept the house until her clothes became dirty."[29]

The hadith further highlights that she did not complain about the matter and that instead of being given help in terms of a servant to do her chores, her noble father ﷺ gave her something far more valuable: 'the *Tasbīḥ* of Sayyidah Fāṭimah'.[30] A similar narration is recorded in *Ṣaḥīḥ Muslim.*[31]

---

[28] The example of Sayyidah Umm ʿAmmārah ﷺ is often cited as 'proof' of feminist ideals being acted out by the Ṣaḥābiyāt ﷺ, but the lack of other named female fighters actually shows that the opposite is true. She was highlighted due to the fact that this was not a common thing to see. It is her exceptional behaviour that makes her stand out in the narrations. If women fighting in the field was commonplace, her name would not have been singled out and there would be far more citable examples of warrior women.

[29] *Sunan Abī Dāwūd*, 2988.

[30] Recital of *Subḥān Allāh* 33 times, *Alḥamdulillāh* 33 times, and *Allāhu Akbar* 34 times, after every *ṣalāh* and before bed.

[31] *Ṣaḥīḥ Muslim*, 2727a.

The above hadiths have been brought forth to show how women earned respect in the time of the Prophet ﷺ—not by being, for all intents and purposes, men with differing physiologies, but being as Allah created them, and being exceptional in this regard. Should you feel any less than a man because of what he does? Ask yourself why society has made you think and feel this way.

Billionaire CEOs and politicians push these ideas of sub-par mass education and women performing all the same roles as men, calling them '50% of the workforce.' Is this because they care about you? Or do they do it to have more people working for them to increase their production and profit capacities? Alongside all this, they have the added bonus of a smaller, more docile, and more controllable population. Allah cares about you more than any of His creation, your mothers included, ever could. He certainly loves you more than the shadowy figures at the top of the capitalist food chain.

4
She is Creative

عَنْ عَائِشَةَ رَضِيَ اللَّهُ عَنْهَا، أَنَّهَا كَانَتْ تَقُولُ:

الشِّعْرُ مِنْهُ حَسَنٌ وَمِنْهُ قَبِيحٌ، خُذْ بِالْحَسَنِ وَدَعِ الْقَبِيحَ، وَلَقَدْ رَوَيْتُ مِنْ شِعْرِ كَعْبِ بْنِ مَالِكٍ أَشْعَارًا، مِنْهَا الْقَصِيدَةُ فِيهَا أَرْبَعُونَ بَيْتًا، وَدُونَ ذَلِكَ.

ʿĀ'ishah ﵂ said:

"In poetry there is both good and bad; take the good and leave the bad. I have related some of the poetry of Kaʿb ibn Mālik, including an ode of forty verses, and some shorter works."[32]

Allah states in the Qur'an:

وَقَرْنَ فِى بُيُوتِكُنَّ وَلَا تَبَرَّجْنَ تَبَرُّجَ ٱلْجَـٰهِلِيَّةِ ٱلْأُولَىٰ ۖ وَأَقِمْنَ ٱلصَّلَوٰةَ وَءَاتِينَ ٱلزَّكَوٰةَ وَأَطِعْنَ ٱللَّهَ وَرَسُولَهُۥٓ ۚ إِنَّمَا يُرِيدُ ٱللَّهُ لِيُذْهِبَ عَنكُمُ ٱلرِّجْسَ أَهْلَ ٱلْبَيْتِ وَيُطَهِّرَكُمْ تَطْهِيرًا

"Settle in your homes, and do not display yourselves as women did in the days of ignorance. Establish prayer, pay alms-tax, and obey Allah and His Messenger. Allah only intends to keep evil away from you and purify you completely, O members of the (Prophet's) family!"[33]

If women are better off not being another body in the workforce, then what should they do with their free time? The obvious answer is to increase one's worship, recite the Qur'an, engage in *dhikr*, send *ṣalawāt* on the Prophet ﷺ and gain a better understanding of the fundamentals of the Faith. However, it would be naive to believe that the majority of women of today would be able to fill their days with strictly worship and spiritual self-betterment. A woman will have spare time on her hands, even if she engages in all of the above *and* fulfils her responsibilities at home as a wife, daughter, and/or mother.

---

[32] Muhammad ibn Ismāʿīl al-Bukhārī, *al-Adab al-Mufrad*, 866.

[33] Qur'an, 33:33.

Across cultures, places, and times, women have engaged in the creative arts as pastimes and have excelled in these fields. Those steeped in western culture will know of the Bronte Sisters and Mary Shelley, of Jane Austen and Maya Angelou, among others. However, these authors and poets pale in comparison to the famed poetesses of Islamic history. Many of the Ṣaḥābiyāt ﷺ were accomplished poets, including Umm al-Mu'minīn Sayyidah ʿĀ'ishah, Umm al-Mu'minīn Sayyidah Ḥafṣah, Sayyidah Fāṭimah, Sayyidah Asmā' bint Abū Bakr, and Sayyidah al-Khansā' ﷺ.[34]

Due to Sharia restrictions on image-creation, sculpting, and music,[35] there is often a misconception that Islamic society does not cater for engaging in the liberal arts. Far from it, Islamic society brought about a golden age of the arts, where creativity and craftsmanship combined to create great intellectual wonders of wordplay, architecture, and art. This began from the era of the Prophet ﷺ. As Umm al-Mu'minīn Sayyidah ʿĀ'ishah ﷺ stated, she herself narrated poetry, and she was a great poet in her own right. Sayyidunā Jābir ibn Samurah ﷺ narrated:

جَالَسْتُ النَّبِيَّ صلى الله عليه وسلم، أَكْثَرَ مِنْ مِائَةِ مَرَّةٍ، وَكَانَ أَصْحَابُهُ يَتَنَاشَدُونَ الشِّعْرَ، وَيَتَذَاكَرُونَ أَشْيَاءَ مِنْ أَمْرِ الْجَاهِلِيَّةِ، وَهُوَ سَاكِتٌ وَرُبَّمَا تَبَسَّمَ مَعَهُمْ.

"I sat with the Prophet ﷺ more than a hundred times. His Ṣaḥābah would recite poetry to one another and reminisce over matters from the Jāhilī Age, while he was silent; sometimes he smiled with them."[36]

The Prophet ﷺ himself listened to and enjoyed good poetry.[37] 'Good' poetry means that the poetry was good in both craftsmanship

---

[34] Sayyidah Tumāḍir bint ʿAmr ibn al-Ḥārith ﷺ, better known as al-Khansā', perhaps deserves the crown of the Queen of Poets for her astounding body of work, which is still read and celebrated by liberal arts scholars and laypeople alike. Regardless, she is without a doubt the finest author of elegies in the Arabic language, and one of the (if not *the*) greatest female authors and poets of all time.

[35] A subject that deserves a book in itself to fully unpack.

[36] Muḥammad ibn ʿĪsā al-Tirmidhī, *al-Shamā'il al-Muḥammadiyyah*, 246.

[37] *Ṣaḥīḥ Muslim*, 2255a, 2255b.

and in meaning. He ﷺ would even quote it sometimes.[38] Sayyidunā Ubayy ibn Kaʿb رضي الله عنه narrated that the Prophet ﷺ said:

إِنَّ مِنَ الشِّعْرِ حِكْمَةً.

"In poetry there is wisdom."[39]

This is not to be understood as a blanket endorsement of poetry. As Umm al-Mu'minīn Sayyidah ʿĀ'ishah رضي الله عنها stated, there is both good and bad poetry. Poetry that is un-Islamic in nature, useless, uncouth, or otherwise considered bad is not a worthwhile pastime. Sayyidunā ʿAbdullāh ibn ʿAmr رضي الله عنه narrated that Allah's Messenger ﷺ said,

الشِّعْرُ بِمَنْزِلَةِ الْكَلامِ حَسَنُهُ كَحَسَنِ الْكَلامِ وَقَبِيحُهُ كَقَبِيحِ الْكَلامِ.

"Poetry is in the same position as speech. Its beauty is like beautiful speech; its ugliness is like ugly speech."[40]

Poetry is not the only creative pastime that is worthwhile, merely the most common one from the Age of Prophethood. Calligraphy, *Tehźīp,*[41] geometric art, architecture, carpentry, stonemasonry, pottery, and so on are all worthwhile endeavours, bringing one joy, allowing one to gain mastery in a field, and to earn some personal income from it. Moreover, it gives every person the chance to benefit the Ummah in some way.

---

[38] *Al-Adab al-Mufrad,* 792.
[39] *Sunan Abī Dāwūd,* 5010.
[40] *Al-Adab al-Mufrad,* 862.
[41] Traditional Turkish/Ottoman Islamic illumination painting.

5
She is a Teacher

عَنْ أَبِي مُوسَى، قَالَ:

مَا أَشْكَلَ عَلَيْنَا أَصْحَابَ رَسُولِ اللَّهِ صلَّى اللَّهُ عَلَيْهِ وَسَلَّمَ حَدِيثٌ قَطُّ فَسَأَلْنَا عَائِشَةَ إِلَّا وَجَدْنَا عِنْدَهَا مِنْهُ عِلْمًا.

Abū Mūsā said:

"We, the Ṣaḥābah of Allah's Messenger ﷺ, never had a problem occur to us except that we would ask ʿĀ'ishah and find that she knew something about it."[42]

Of all the students of the Prophet ﷺ, Umm al-Mu'minīn Sayyidah ʿĀ'ishah ؓ had the greatest access to his knowledge on account of being his beloved wife. She was with him at times when no one else was present, internalised many of his teachings, and narrated thousands of hadiths from him. She was known amongst the Ṣaḥābah ؓ as a jurist and a teacher.

In Islamic society, teaching and learning are two of the noblest pursuits a Muslim can undertake. This is no different for either gender. It should, however, be noted and understood here that the 'education' being discussed is knowledge of the *Dīn*, and not the secularised liberal education that we often see people try to prioritise in the Western world. In a society with traditional roles and norms, there is no need or requirement for a woman to learn to become an electrician, firefighter, a scientist, or a CEO. This is only useful for a society that wishes to maximise its 'workforce' for financial gain, not for a society that wishes to maximise *taqwā* for spiritual gain. As Muslims, our womenfolk are encouraged to gain Islamic knowledge and teach it to others.

---

[42] *Jāmiʿ al-Tirmidhī*, 3883.

A woman is the primary tutor of her children, and as the saying goes 'the mother is the first *madrasah*'. As women, this is a sacred duty and of great reward. Every noble quality instilled in your children, every Islamic discipline or practice conveyed to them to act upon and pass forward will become a *ṣadaqah jāriyah* (a perpetual charity) for the woman who taught them. In this way, there can be nothing more profitable than a woman teaching her children the basic tenets of faith and the Arabic alphabet; their every act of worship will accrue reward for her and she will have the peace of mind of knowing her children are safe in their faith.

Too often the task of educating our children is given to others. We are content in our subscription to a society that advocates for two working parents to send their children to people who disagree with them on *the most fundamental matters:* on the existence of God and His nature, on what is right and wrong, and what our purpose in life is. We cannot do this for 18 years and then wonder why our children think so differently to us or, Allah forbid, are even leaving the fold of Islam. When we prioritise money over the faith of our own children, can there be a more despicable group of people? We each choose what we value most, make our decisions in life based on those things, and then live with the consequences.

A woman should thus seek knowledge that benefits her role in Islamic society. She should learn virtue and morals, *fiqh* and *aqīdah* and hadith such as those found in the *Arbaʿīn* of Imām al-Nawawī ﵀ (and, dare I say, this book and its companion), and she should memorise and learn the Qur'an. She can then teach her children, her sisters, and her elders, and strengthen Islam in her life and the lives of others. Umm al-Mu'minīn Sayyidah ʿĀ'ishah ﵂ narrated from Allah's Messenger ﷺ:

$$\text{مُعَلِّمُ الْخَيْرِ يَسْتَغْفِرُ لَهُ كُلُّ شَيْءٍ حَتَّى الْحِيتَانُ فِي الْبَحْرِ}$$

"Everything seeks forgiveness for the teacher of virtue, even the fish in the sea."[43]

There is no restriction on what beneficial knowledge she can gather and pass on to others. Sayyidunā ʿUrwah narrated:

$$\text{عَنْ عَائِشَةَ - رضى الله عنها - أَنَّهَا كَانَتْ تَأْمُرُ بِالتَّلْبِينِ لِلْمَرِيضِ وَلِلْمَحْزُونِ عَلَى الْهَالِكِ، وَكَانَتْ تَقُولُ إِنِّي سَمِعْتُ رَسُولَ اللهِ صلى الله عليه وسلم يَقُولُ: إِنَّ التَّلْبِينَةَ تُجِمُّ فُؤَادَ الْمَرِيضِ، وَتَذْهَبُ بِبَعْضِ الْحُزْنِ.}$$

"Umm al-Mu'minīn Sayyidah ʿĀ'ishah used to recommend talbīnah[44] for the sick and those grieving the dead. She would say, 'I heard Allah's Messenger saying, "Talbīnah strengthens the patient's heart and makes it active and relieves some of his grief."'"[45]

Sayyidunā ʿUrwah was the son of Sayyidunā al-Zubayr ibn al-ʿAwwām and Sayyidah Asmā' bint Abū Bakr, and the nephew of Umm al-Mu'minīn Sayyidah ʿĀ'ishah, and thus she was able to teach him directly. Similarly, Sayyidah Umm Qays bint Miḥṣan narrated that she heard Allah's Messenger say:

$$\text{عَلَيْكُمْ بِهَذَا الْعُودِ الْهِنْدِيِّ، فَإِنَّ فِيهِ سَبْعَةَ أَشْفِيَةٍ. يُسْتَعَطُ بِهِ مِنَ الْعُذْرَةِ، وَيُلَدُّ بِهِ مِنْ ذَاتِ الْجَنْبِ.}$$

"Treat (patients) with Indian incense, for it is a cure for seven diseases. It can be sniffed by one whose throat troubles him, and can be placed in the side of the mouth of one suffering from pleurisy."[46]

So, learn and then teach. Prioritise what you learn, and whom you teach. Remember, a woman teaches as much by example as with her words; she cannot teach the primacy of the Hereafter with her tongue but exhibit subservience to the world with her actions. Having read the

---

[43] Abū Bakr Aḥmad al-Bazzār, *Musnad al-Bazzār*, 169.
[44] A traditional dish made of barley, milk, water, and honey.
[45] *Ṣaḥīḥ al-Bukhārī*, 5689.
[46] *Ṣaḥīḥ al-Bukhārī*, 5692, 5693.

above, should you still choose to send your children to non-Muslim schools, know what you are teaching them with your own actions: that you are sending them to someone who knows better than you. Do not be surprised when they take their lessons over yours.

6
She Chooses Words Wisely

عَنْ أُمِّ عُمَارَةَ الْأَنْصَارِيَّةِ أَنَّهَا أَتَتْ النَّبِيَّ ﷺ فَقَالَتْ مَا أَرَى كُلَّ شَيْءٍ إِلَّا لِلرِّجَالِ وَمَا
أَرَى النِّسَاءَ يُذْكَرْنَ بِشَيْءٍ فَنَزَلَتْ هَذِهِ الْآيَةَ:

إِنَّ الْمُسْلِمِينَ وَالْمُسْلِمَاتِ وَالْمُؤْمِنِينَ وَالْمُؤْمِنَاتِ وَالْقَانِتِينَ وَالْقَانِتَاتِ وَالصَّادِقِينَ
وَالصَّادِقَاتِ وَالصَّابِرِينَ وَالصَّابِرَاتِ وَالْخَاشِعِينَ وَالْخَاشِعَاتِ وَالْمُتَصَدِّقِينَ وَالْمُتَصَدِّقَاتِ
وَالصَّائِمِينَ وَالصَّائِمَاتِ وَالْحَافِظِينَ فُرُوجَهُمْ وَالْحَافِظَاتِ وَالذَّاكِرِينَ اللَّهَ كَثِيرًا وَالذَّاكِرَاتِ
أَعَدَّ اللَّهُ لَهُم مَّغْفِرَةً وَأَجْرًا عَظِيمًا.

Umm ʿUmārah ﵂ narrated that she came to the Prophet ﷺ and said, "I see nothing except that it is for men; I see nothing mentioned for women." This *āyah* was then revealed:[47]

"Indeed, the Muslim men and Muslim women, the believing men and believing women, the obedient men and obedient women, the truthful men and truthful women, the patient men and patient women, the humble men and humble women, the charitable men and charitable women, the fasting men and fasting women, the men who guard their private parts and the women who do so, and the men who remember Allah often and the women who do so – for them Allah has prepared forgiveness and a great reward."[48]

When used correctly, concise, purposeful words are extremely powerful. What a woman lacks in physical strength and power she can make up for through the eloquence of her speech. Many a melancholy heart has been warmed by a few choice words, and many an angry soul has been soothed by the same. Sayyidunā Ibn ʿAbbās ﵄ narrated:

---

[47] *Jāmiʿ al-Tirmidhī*, 3211.
[48] Qur'an, 33:35.

أَنَّ رَجُلاً، أَوْ أَعْرَابِيًّا، أَتَى النَّبِيَّ صلى الله عليه وسلم فَتَكَلَّمَ بِكَلاَمٍ بَيِّنٍ، فَقَالَ النَّبِيُّ صلى الله عليه وسلم: إِنَّ مِنَ الْبَيَانِ سِحْرًا، وَإِنَّ مِنَ الشِّعْرِ حِكْمَةً.

> "A man – or a Bedouin – came to the Prophet ﷺ and spoke eloquently. The Prophet ﷺ said, 'In eloquence there is magic and in poetry there is wisdom.'"[49]

In the narration of Sayyidah Umm 'Umārah ؓ, her eloquence was on full display. Her words, though terse, became the reason for the revelation of an *āyah*. This is the power of speech. In fact, eloquent speech was one of the blessings that Allah bestowed upon the Prophet ﷺ, giving him a great advantage over his enemies. Sayyidunā Abū Hurayrah ؓ narrated that the Prophet ﷺ said,

أُعْطِيتُ مَفَاتِيحَ الْكَلِمِ، وَنُصِرْتُ بِالرُّعْبِ.

> "I have been granted the keys of eloquence and granted victory through awe."[50]

A woman should be capable of using eloquent speech to convince others of her arguments. Though she cannot resort to brute force to create change, Islam does not dictate that a woman cannot speak when she needs to. Yet eloquence alone is not inherently a good thing. The tongue is a double-edged sword, and it must be treated as such. If used correctly, it is the weapon of a believer, but if used uncaringly it is a weapon against you. It must not be drawn unless required, and when drawn it must strike its target and then return to its scabbard. Sayyidunā Sahl ibn Sa'd ؓ narrated that Allah's Messenger ﷺ said,

مَنْ يَضْمَنْ لِي مَا بَيْنَ لَحْيَيْهِ وَمَا بَيْنَ رِجْلَيْهِ أَضْمَنْ لَهُ الْجَنَّةَ.

> "Whoever gives guarantee of what is between his jawbones and what is between his legs, I guarantee him Paradise."[51]

---

[49] *Al-Adab al-Mufrad*, 872.
[50] *Ṣaḥīḥ al-Bukhārī*, 6998.
[51] *Ṣaḥīḥ al-Bukhārī*, 6474.

Guarding one's tongue is equally important to chastity in guaranteeing our Hereafter. Too often, this is taken lightly but it is a grave matter. How many of us snap at our family members and friends, or say hurtful words, without considering the consequences? Being angry is not an excuse. It is not a difficult thing to hold your tongue in check, yet the consequences of not doing so can be catastrophic for the speaker.

Equally important is ensuring that the words one speaks are truthful, even if harm is neither meant nor caused. Sayyidah Asmā' bint Yazīd ؓ narrated:

أُتِيَ النَّبِيُّ ﷺ بِطَعَامٍ فَعَرَضَ عَلَيْنَا فَقُلْنَا: لَا نَشْتَهِيهِ. فَقَالَ: لَا تَجْمَعْنَ جُوعًا وَكَذِبًا.

"Food was brought to the Prophet ﷺ and he presented it before us. We said, 'We have no appetite.' The Prophet ﷺ said, 'Do not combine hunger with lies.'"[52]

Combining hunger with dishonesty refers to the fact that they refused the food, despite being hungry.[53] It may seem a trivial thing to modern eyes and ears, and, generally speaking, the women were being modest and proper in not wanting to eat, but even in this situation honesty cannot be compromised for the sake of propriety. It is therefore better not to speak than to say something false. Allah says:

إِذْ تَلَقَّوْنَهُ بِأَلْسِنَتِكُمْ وَتَقُولُونَ بِأَفْوَاهِكُم مَّا لَيْسَ لَكُم بِهِ عِلْمٌ وَتَحْسَبُونَهُ هَيِّنًا وَهُوَ عِندَ اللَّهِ عَظِيمٌ (١٥)

When you passed it from one tongue to the other, and said with your mouths what you had no knowledge of, taking it lightly while it is serious in the sight of Allah.[54]

---

[52] Abū 'Abdullāh Muhammad ibn Yazīd ibn Mājah al-Rab'ī al-Qazwīnī, *Sunan Ibn Mājah*, 3298.
[53] 'Alī ibn Sulṭān Muhammad al-Harawī al-Qārī, *Mirqāt al-Mafātīḥ*, 4256.
[54] Qur'an, 24:15.

It is no small thing to speak untruths. Regarding the above verse, Sayyidunā Ibn Abū Mulaykah ﵁ narrated:

عَنْ عَائِشَةَ - رضى الله عنها - كَانَتْ تَقْرَأُ {إِذْ تَلِقُونَهُ بِأَلْسِنَتِكُمْ} وَتَقُولُ الْوَلْقُ الْكَذِبُ.

"Ā'ishah ﵂ used to recite the verse, 'When you passed it from one tongue to the other...'[55] and would say that 'al-walq' means 'to lie'."[56]

Untruths must not be spread, nor should gossip be carried between people. Umm Jamīl, the *kāfir* wife of Abū Lahab, who was damned alongside him in Sūrah al-Masad[57] is referred to in the verses:

وَٱمْرَأَتُهُۥ حَمَّالَةَ ٱلْحَطَبِ (٤) فِى جِيدِهَا حَبْلٌ مِّن مَّسَدٍۭ (٥)

"And his wife, the carrier of kindling. Around her neck is a rope of [twisted] fibre."[58]

The phrase '*al-ḥaṭab*' or 'firewood' was used to refer to slander and gossip amongst the Arabs, likely due to rumours 'catching fire' and spreading quickly, causing great harm.[59] Umm Jamīl would literally throw thorny branches in the path of the Prophet ﷺ and figuratively do so by spreading lies and rumours.[60] For this behaviour she was damned to Hell.

Even when the information is true, it should still not be spread unless greater harm could be caused by not divulging it. A woman should be the trustworthy confidante of her loved ones. Confidentiality and discretion are essential to earning and keeping someone's trust. If she is quick to tell people the secrets of others, she cannot be trusted.

---

[55] ibid.

[56] *Ṣaḥīḥ al-Bukhārī*, 4144.

[57] Interestingly, all either of them had to do to disprove Islam was to accept Islam, as the *sūrah* had been revealed very early on. If they had accepted Islam, the Qur'an would have been proven false due to the paradoxical nature of salvation and forgiveness when accepting Islam when coupled with being named in the Qur'an as being damned. This in itself is a proof of the Truth of the Qur'an and Islam.

[58] Qur'an, 111:4-5.

[59] Muhammad Shafīʿ al-ʿUthmānī, *Maʿārif al-Qur'ān*, vol. 8, p. 911.

[60] ibid.

A major reason why marriages fall apart in modern society is because spouses cannot keep their disputes confidential; every little gripe or issue is passed on to family members, who then become involved in the dispute and the fire spreads until it consumes the relationship and burns away all good will. Sayyidunā Jābir ibn ʿAbdullāh ﷺ narrated that Allah's Messenger ﷺ said:

الْمَجَالِسُ بِالأَمَانَةِ إِلاَّ ثَلاَثَةَ مَجَالِسَ سَفْكُ دَمٍ حَرَامٍ أَوْ فَرْجٌ حَرَامٌ أَوِ اقْتِطَاعُ مَالٍ بِغَيْرِ حَقٍّ.

"All meetings are confidential except three: those for shedding unlawful blood, for unlawful sex, or for the unjust taking of property."[61]

Essentially, if the meeting is not related to the planning or execution of a crime, its contents should not be divulged to another.

It should also be noted that when people are sitting together, care should be taken to ensure that individuals are not singled out or excluded from the conversation. This is an example of extremely poor manners and etiquette, and is even a means of earning the displeasure of Allah. Sayyidunā Ibn ʿAbbās ﷺ narrated that Allah's Messenger ﷺ said:

لاَ يَتَنَاجَى اثْنَانِ دُونَ الثَّالِثِ فَإِنَّ ذَلِكَ يُؤْذِي الْمُؤْمِنَ وَاللَّهُ تَعَالَى يَكْرَهُ أَذَى الْمُؤْمِنِ.

"Let not two converse privately while excluding the third, for that will hurt the believer. Allah the Exalted dislikes the believer's pain."[62]

This refers to all forms of exclusion, including speaking with one another and ignoring the third person, not acknowledging the third person when they join the gathering, whispering to hide what is being said from the third person, and switching to a language that the third person does not understand to exclude them.

---

[61] *Sunan Abī Dāwūd*, 4869.

[62] Sulaymān ibn Aḥmad ibn Ayyūb ibn Muṭayyir al-Ṭabarānī, *al-Muʿjam al-Awsaṭ*, 1986.

Remember: a blunt tongue is useless, a sharp tongue used surgically can benefit, and a tongue used as a weapon can harm others and oneself. Words can be medicine or poison; use them wisely.

7
She Judges Not

عَنْ عَائِشَةَ عَنْ رَسُولِ اللهِ صَلَّى اللهُ عَلَيْهِ وَسَلَّمَ أَنَّهُ قَالَ أَتَدْرُونَ مَنْ السَّابِقُونَ إِلَى ظِلِّ اللهِ عَزَّ وَجَلَّ يَوْمَ الْقِيَامَةِ؟ قَالُوا اللهُ وَرَسُولُهُ أَعْلَمُ. قَالَ الَّذِينَ إِذَا أُعْطُوا الْحَقَّ قَبِلُوهُ وَإِذَا سُئِلُوهُ بَذَلُوهُ وَحَكَمُوا لِلنَّاسِ كَحُكْمِهِمْ لِأَنْفُسِهِمْ

ʿĀ'ishah narrated that Allah's Messenger ﷺ asked, "Do you know who are the forerunners to the shade of Allah the Mighty and Majestic on the Day of Resurrection?" The Ṣaḥābah replied, "Allah and His Messenger know best." The Prophet ﷺ said, "They are those who accept the truth when they receive it and offer it when they are asked for it, and judge people the way they judge themselves."[68]

A woman is not harsh with others, nor is she judgemental. In modern times, it has become somewhat of a cliché that women are quick to judge each other, however in the time of the Prophet ﷺ this was not so. As Muslims, our behaviour should not be harsh with one another. The proverb 'Treat others as you would like to be treated' is a universal sentiment across all creeds and cultures, and Islam is no different. Allah's Messenger ﷺ advised that, as Muslims, it is our duty with regard to other Muslims that we love for them what we love for ourselves.[64]

When we see our fellow Muslims have slipped, made a mistake, or fallen into what appears to be falsehood, we should not judge them. In fact, we should make excuses for them in our hearts to ensure we maintain a good idea of them. Were we to be in the same situation, we would not want others to think badly of us, even if what they thought was true. Why then should we expect or wish for one standard for ourselves, and another for our sisters? Allah says in the Qur'an:

---

[63] *Musnad al-Imām Aḥmad*, 24379.
[64] *Jāmiʿ al-Tirmidhī*, 2736.

يَـٰٓأَيُّهَا ٱلَّذِينَ ءَامَنُوا۟ لَا يَسْخَرْ قَوْمٌ مِّن قَوْمٍ عَسَىٰٓ أَن يَكُونُوا۟ خَيْرًا مِّنْهُمْ وَلَا نِسَآءٌ مِّن نِّسَآءٍ عَسَىٰٓ أَن يَكُنَّ خَيْرًا مِّنْهُنَّ ۖ وَلَا تَلْمِزُوٓا۟ أَنفُسَكُمْ وَلَا تَنَابَزُوا۟ بِٱلْأَلْقَـٰبِ ۖ بِئْسَ ٱلِٱسْمُ ٱلْفُسُوقُ بَعْدَ ٱلْإِيمَـٰنِ ۚ وَمَن لَّمْ يَتُبْ فَأُو۟لَـٰٓئِكَ هُمُ ٱلظَّـٰلِمُونَ (١١)

"O believers! Do not let some [men] ridicule others, they may be better than them, nor let women ridicule other women, they may be better than them. Do not defame one another, nor call each other by offensive nicknames. How evil it is to act rebelliously after having faith! And whoever does not repent, it is they who are the wrongdoers."[65]

It may just be the case that this person you are ridiculing and judging is closer to Allah than you are, and thus more deserving of salvation in the Hereafter. The *āyah* above prohibits ridiculing others, defaming them, and even giving them offensive names. It is often too easy to look towards the faults of others, and be blind to our own shortcomings. One should focus on their own faults whenever their eyes fall upon the faults of others. As the last emperor of India, Bahādur Shāh Zafar ﷀ stated:

نہ تھی حال کی جب ہمیں اپنی خبر رہے دیکھتے لوگوں کے عیب و ہنر

پڑی اپنی برائیوں پر جو نظر تو جہان میں کوئی بُرا نہ رہا

When unaware of our internal ails,

Then all that we could see was others fail;

When faults of ours then fell beneath our sight,

The world was never wrong and ever right.

Secondly, a woman should accept the truth when she receives it, regardless of the source of that truth. If a sister you have disagreements with is offering you sound advice, whether sincere or otherwise, it is up to you as a Muslimah to take the truth and accept it. Likewise, when giving advice, if someone asks for the truth from you it should never be the case that the truth is hidden from them in an attempt to save

---

[65] Qur'an, 49:11.

face or protect feelings. Lying is lying, and a Muslimah does not engage in such. However, this does not mean that a woman should deliver the truth to her sister in a harsh manner. Even a harsh truth can be delivered with kindness and compassion, and here again eloquence has its role to play. Honest advice, soundly given, is more likely to be accepted by others.

Be kind in what you say and how you say it, but do not move away from the truth. Have a care for the feelings of others, especially your sisters, who are equally as sensitive and empathetic as you are, but balance this with honesty in your advice and opinions; giving unsound advice or a false opinion is a way to cause harm to others and not becoming of a Muslim.

8
She is Resilient

عَنْ عَطَاءِ بْنِ أَبِي رَبَاحٍ، قَالَ:

قَالَ لِي ابْنُ عَبَّاسٍ: أَلاَ أُرِيكَ امْرَأَةً مِنْ أَهْلِ الْجَنَّةِ؟ قُلْتُ: بَلَى. قَالَ: هَذِهِ الْمَرْأَةُ السَّوْدَاءُ أَتَتِ النَّبِيَّ صلى الله عليه وسلم فَقَالَتْ: إِنِّي أُصْرَعُ، وَإِنِّي أَتَكَشَّفُ فَادْعُ اللَّهَ لِي. قَالَ: إِنْ شِئْتِ صَبَرْتِ وَلَكِ الْجَنَّةُ، وَإِنْ شِئْتِ دَعَوْتُ اللَّهَ أَنْ يُعَافِيَكِ. فَقَالَتْ: أَصْبِرُ. فَقَالَتْ: إِنِّي أَتَكَشَّفُ فَادْعُ اللَّهَ أَنْ لاَ أَتَكَشَّفَ، فَدَعَا لَهَا.

عَنِ ابْنِ جُرَيْجٍ، أَخْبَرَنِي عَطَاءٌ، أَنَّهُ رَأَى أُمَّ زُفَرَ تِلْكَ امْرَأَةٌ طَوِيلَةٌ سَوْدَاءُ عَلَى سِتْرِ الْكَعْبَةِ.

ʿAṭāʾ ibn Abī Rabāḥ narrates:

"Ibn ʿAbbās said to me, 'Shall I show you a woman from the people of Paradise?' I said, 'Of course.' He said, 'This black lady came to the Prophet ﷺ and said, "I suffer from epilepsy and my body becomes uncovered; please pray to Allah for me." The Prophet ﷺ said, "If you wish, be patient and you will have Paradise; and if you wish, I will pray to Allah to cure you." She said, "I will remain patient." Then she added, "But I become uncovered, so please pray to Allah on my behalf so that I may not become uncovered." So he prayed to Allah for her.'"

Ibn Jurayj narrated that ʿAṭāʾ told him he had seen Umm Zufar, the tall black lady, clinging to the curtain of the Kaʿbah.[66]

In the modern era, it has become the case that the word 'strength' has become androgynous, losing all its nuance. The strength of a woman is, supposedly, to be compared with the strength of a man. If men can lift large, heavy objects then women can too; if men are courageous in the battlefield, then women are too; if a man can work on an oil rig in the North Atlantic, then women can too. Women's so-called empowerment appears to be entirely based on a false

[66] *Ṣaḥīḥ al-Bukhārī,* 5652.

comparison and equivalency to men, as if there is only one kind of courage and one kind of strength. This foolishness has mutated over the years since the feminist movement first emerged and has now become rampant within the ranks of the Muslims as well. We are quick to latch onto stories of women who showed bravery in the battlefield, such as Sayyidah Umm ʿAmmārah ﵂ in the battle of Uḥud, not realising that her courage in the field of battle was noteworthy due to its rarity; it was the exception rather than the rule.

The idea that there is only one form of courage or strength is false. A strong woman is not a strong man with ovaries. It is high time that the women of the Ummah learned again that there is such a thing as feminine courage, bravery, and strength, that women can and should volunteer to help where the laws of Islam allow, and that the resilience of women has its own noble place in the eyes of the Ummah. This resilience, though different to the resilience and steadfastness of men, is no less praiseworthy. A woman does not have to be equal to a man in Islam; she need only strive to be equal to her fellow women.

In the above narration, Sayyidah Umm Zufar ﵂ showed extreme patience in the face of a life-long debilitating illness, choosing to bear her suffering with patience for the reward promised to her by the Prophet ﷺ in the Hereafter. She remained principled and disciplined, and when she had heard what the Prophet ﷺ had to say, her concern was no longer with regard to the epilepsy and its effects on her, but on the uncovering of her body during the ordeals. Her resilience, courage, and even her concern, were uniquely feminine in nature. Is such an example of patience in the face of life-long suffering any less courageous than those of her fellow Ṣaḥābah ﵃ who faced foes in the field of war? It is a different kind of courage, but she was no less brave.

There are many examples of resilience and patience in the stories of the Ṣaḥābah ﵃. Umm al-Mu'minīn Sayyidah Umm Salamah ﵂ narrates:

لَمَّا مَاتَ أَبُو سَلَمَةَ، قُلْتُ: غَرِيبٌ وَفِي أَرْضِ غُرْبَةٍ، لأَبْكِيَنَّهُ بُكَاءً يُتَحَدَّثُ عَنْهُ. فَكُنْتُ قَدْ تَهَيَّأْتُ لِلْبُكَاءِ عَلَيْهِ إِذْ أَقْبَلَتِ امْرَأَةٌ مِنَ الصَّعِيدِ تُرِيدُ أَنْ تُسْعِدَنِي فَاسْتَقْبَلَهَا رَسُولُ اللَّهِ

صلى الله عليه وسلم وَقَالَ أَتُرِيدِينَ أَنْ تُدْخِلِي الشَّيْطَانَ بَيْتًا أَخْرَجَهُ اللهُ مِنْهُ مَرَّتَيْنِ فَكَفَفْتُ عَنِ الْبُكَاءِ فَلَمْ أَبْكِ.

"When Abū Salamah died I said, 'I am a stranger in a strange land. I shall weep for him in a manner that will be talked of.' I was preparing to weep for him when a woman from the upper side of the city arrived who had intended to help me. She came across Allah's Messenger ﷺ and he said to her, 'Do you intend to enter the Shayṭān into a house from which Allah has twice removed him?' I therefore refrained from weeping and did not weep."[67]

Umm al-Mu'minīn Sayyidah Umm Salamah ﵂ was far from home and grieving for her husband at the time. She had suffered many years at the hands of the Polytheists following her acceptance of Islam and the story of her separation from her husband and her child is well-known to all. Despite the hardships she had endured and the grief that she was suffering from at the time, the advice of the Prophet ﷺ was sufficient for her. She refrained from weeping and grieved for her husband as was befitting her rank and status. She would soon be rewarded for her patience when she was granted a husband far greater than even Sayyidunā Abū Salamah ﵁: Allah's Messenger ﷺ himself.

Patience and resilience, then, can be seen as forms of strength and bravery that women can engage and excel in. This is not to say that women cannot or should not play their parts on the battlefield when there is a requirement, only that even here there is no need to compare one's courage and contribution with that of one's male counterparts. A field medic, a water carrier, or a stretcher-bearer is no less brave than the man holding the spear or the sword. Sayyidah Rubayyiʿ bint Muʿawwidh ibn ʿAfraʾ ﵂ narrates in *Ṣaḥīḥ al-Bukhārī*:

كُنَّا نَغْزُو مَعَ رَسُولِ اللَّهِ صلى الله عليه وسلم نَسْقِي الْقَوْمَ، وَنَخْدُمُهُمْ، وَنَرُدُّ الْقَتْلَى وَالْجَرْحَى إِلَى الْمَدِينَةِ.

[67] *Ṣaḥīḥ Muslim*, 922.

"We used to go for military expeditions along with Allah's Messenger ﷺ, providing the people with water, serving them, and bringing the dead and wounded back to Madinah."[68]

She also narrated:

كُنَّا مَعَ النَّبِيِّ صلى الله عليه وسلم نَسْقِي، وَنُدَاوِي الْجَرْحَى، وَنَرُدُّ الْقَتْلَى إِلَى الْمَدِينَةِ.

"We were with the Prophet ﷺ, providing water, treating the wounded, and returning the slain to Madinah."[69]

A woman's strength lies in her resilience and her patience. Do not measure your worth by how you compare with men, but seek instead to see how close you are to the examples of these great women.

---

[68] *Ṣaḥīḥ al-Bukhārī*, 5679.
[69] *Ṣaḥīḥ al-Bukhārī*, 2882.

9
She is a Gracious Host

عَنْ عَائِشَةَ أَنَّ النَّبِيَّ صَلَّى اللهُ عَلَيْهِ وَسَلَّمَ قَالَ:

إِنَّهُ مَنْ أُعْطِيَ حَظَّهُ مِنَ الرِّفْقِ فَقَدْ أُعْطِيَ حَظَّهُ مِنْ خَيْرِ الدُّنْيَا وَالْآخِرَةِ وَصِلَةُ الرَّحِمِ وَحُسْنُ الْخُلُقِ وَحُسْنُ الْجِوَارِ يَعْمُرَانِ الدِّيَارَ وَيَزِيدَانِ فِي الْأَعْمَارِ.

ʿĀ'ishah narrated that the Prophet ﷺ said:

"Indeed, whoever has been given the quality of kindness has been given their share of good in the world and the Hereafter. Maintaining family ties, good character, and good neighbourliness will build their heavenly abodes and increase their lives."[70]

A woman's domain is within the walls of her home. It is her responsibility to care for it and those within its borders, nurturing them and supporting them to become the best they can be, while becoming the best version of herself in the process. This does not preclude her ability to engage with the outside world in a meaningful way, as the outside world comes to her, giving her the opportunity to display the heavenly goodness she has been granted in the form of her inherent kindness and hospitality.

Hospitality and guest rights are an important aspect of Islamic society; they are the cement that holds together the bricks of the family unit, and are essential to building a strong and interdependent society. Women have been created to be sociable, and sociability is often an intrinsic part of who they are. The Islamic way of life takes people as they are and guides them to the correct usage of their talents and natural inclinations, rather than merely prohibiting and restricting them from using these gifts. As such, women are encouraged to show hospitality and look after their guests, providing them with food and drink, and hosting and treating their female neighbours well. Neighbourliness and sociability are core components of good

---

[70] *Musnad al-Imām Aḥmad*, 25259.

character, and the reward for such goodness is greater goodness in the Hereafter. How beautiful Islam is! Be sociable and kind with your neighbours in your worldly abode; gain blessing in your worldly life and far greater abodes in Heaven, in which you may *in shā Allāh* host those same neighbours again one day.

So important is the task of caring for our neighbours and their well-treatment, that Umm al-Mu'minīn Sayyidah ʿĀ'ishah narrated that the Prophet ﷺ said:

مَا زَالَ يُوصِينِي جِبْرِيلُ بِالْجَارِ حَتَّى ظَنَنْتُ أَنَّهُ سَيُوَرِّثُهُ

"Jibrīl continued to instruct me to treat neighbours well to the extent that I thought he would make them heirs."[71]

That is to say, Sayyidunā Jibrīl highlighted their well-treatment to such an extent that the Prophet ﷺ expected him to say that they should be included in one's will and have a share in the inheritance.

In reality, good treatment of our neighbours is not difficult. Smile when you see them, give them *salām*, offer them aid when they need it, share food with one another, and visit each other's houses. Sayyidunā Abū Dharr narrated:

إِنَّ خَلِيلِي صلى الله عليه وسلم أَوْصَانِي:

"إِذَا طَبَخْتَ مَرَقًا فَأَكْثِرْ مَاءَهُ ثُمَّ انْظُرْ أَهْلَ بَيْتٍ مِنْ جِيرَانِكَ فَأَصِبْهُمْ مِنْهَا بِمَعْرُوفٍ."

"My dear friend (Allah's Messenger ﷺ) advised me:

'When you prepare a broth, increase it by adding water, then look to the members of your neighbouring households and courteously give to them from this.'"[72]

Acting upon this advice means that you are not decreasing your own food at all, but increasing your ability to share it, thereby feeding more people, building love and strong ties within your community, and

---

[71] *Ṣaḥīḥ al-Bukhārī*, 6014; *Ṣaḥīḥ Muslim*, 2624.
[72] *Ṣaḥīḥ Muslim*, 2625c.

increasing the blessings of Allah upon you. Being a gracious host is not difficult for the woman whose heart is clean.

10
She is Courteous

عَنْ أَبِي هُرَيْرَةَ، عَنِ النَّبِيِّ صلى الله عليه وسلم قَالَ:
لَوْ كُنْتُ آمِرًا أَحَدًا أَنْ يَسْجُدَ لِأَحَدٍ لَأَمَرْتُ الْمَرْأَةَ أَنْ تَسْجُدَ لِزَوْجِهَا.

Abū Hurayrah narrated that the Prophet said:

"Were I to order anyone to prostrate to anyone, I would order the wife to prostrate to her husband."[73]

Courtesy and respect go hand in hand. Globally, they are desired qualities in womenfolk, pointing towards a correlation with *fiṭrah*. Men find women who are respectful and courteous to be more desirable partners, and it is no wonder why. A woman who gives due respect and has good, courteous manners will appreciate the work her husband does for her. From a woman's perspective, honouring one's partner in this way will lead to a healthier relationship and will breed a like-for-like exchange where her male counterpart will also become more courteous and appreciative as a result. There are of course exceptions to this, as all men are not angelic by nature, but this is not due to any failing found with courtesy itself but due rather to choosing a poor life-partner to begin with.

In the above narration, the statement of the Prophet should be understood in context. Prostration or even bowing to anyone as a means of worship or thanks is not permissible in Islam, and therefore the hadith can cause confusion if not properly understood. The Prophet used the term *if*, implying a hypothetical context, to highlight the level of respect that a woman should have for her husband, meaning that she should have the highest possible respect for her husband that does not fall into the category of worship. Devotion is a much sought-after quality in a wife, regardless of a man's culture or

---

[73] *Jāmiʿ al-Tirmidhī*, 1159.

creed, and here we can see that the Prophet ﷺ advised women to be devoted to their husbands, showing the greatest possible love and respect for them. It is a tragedy to see certain women treating their line managers with such admiration and devotion, while they treat their husbands with nothing but contempt.

Having said this, courtesy and respect are not exclusive to one's husband, nor is it only women that are required to exhibit these qualities. Sayyidunā ʿAlī ؓ narrated that Allah's Messenger ﷺ said:

لِلْمُسْلِمِ عَلَى الْمُسْلِمِ سِتٌّ بِالْمَعْرُوفِ: يُسَلِّمُ عَلَيْهِ إِذَا لَقِيَهُ وَيُجِيبُهُ إِذَا دَعَاهُ وَيُشَمِّتُهُ إِذَا عَطَسَ وَيَعُودُهُ إِذَا مَرِضَ وَيَتْبَعُ جَنَازَتَهُ إِذَا مَاتَ وَيُحِبُّ لَهُ مَا يُحِبُّ لِنَفْسِهِ.

"Six courtesies are due from one Muslim to another: To give salām when he meets him, to accept his invitation, to reply when he sneezes, to visit when he is ill, to attend his funeral, and to love for him what he loves for himself."[74]

These are the basics. They are the baseline courtesies that a Muslim *must* give to another Muslim. When a Muslim offers you the greeting of peace, you must return it. How many of us, when upset with our brothers and sisters, refuse to reply? It is the same with other prayers that Muslims exchange with each other, such as replying to a sneeze. Again, we find that the ones that dislike their sisters choose to ignore this Sunnah, not realising it is their right as Muslims. This is not becoming of a Muslim. Likewise, when we are invited to someone's home or offered food, we should accept their offer, as refusing to do so is disrespectful. When they are ill, we should visit them. At the very least, using the ease provided by today's technology, we should send them a message or give them a call. Love for each other what you love for yourself is a universal concept that does not need further unpacking. In another hadith, Sayyidunā Ibn ʿAbbās ؓ narrated that Allah's Messenger ﷺ said,

لَيْسَ مِنَّا مَنْ لَمْ يَرْحَمْ صَغِيرَنَا وَيُوَقِّرْ كَبِيرَنَا وَيَأْمُرْ بِالْمَعْرُوفِ وَيَنْهَ عَنِ الْمُنْكَرِ.

---

[74] *Jāmiʿ al-Tirmidhī*, 2736.

"Whoever has no mercy upon our young, nor respect for our elders, and does not command good and forbid evil is not from amongst us."[75]

Courtesy is not just for those who are our social equals, such as other womenfolk of similar social standing, nor just for those who command our respect due to their lofty position, such as one's husband, ruler, or a scholar of Islam. Courtesy is due to every member of Islamic society, including the most vulnerable amongst us: the children and the elderly. We should show children courtesy by dealing with them with mercy and affection, guiding them with care and attention, and making them feel safe and loved.

The elderly should be given respect. Whether they are noble people worthy of respect on merit, or ignoble people who have attained old age, respect is their due. They have lived long and are nearing the end of their short time on this Earth, and for the young to take this courtesy away from them says more about the young person than the elderly. Deal with them kindly and make the last of their days comfortable, for they are preparing for the journey that we all must take and a good word from them could be the reason for you arriving at your desired destination.

Furthermore, it would be remiss not to state that even universal rights have their exceptions. Sayyidunā Qatādah ﵀ narrated that Sayyidunā al-Ḥasan ﵁ said,

لَيْسَ بَيْنَكَ وَبَيْنَ الْفَاسِقِ حُرْمَةٌ.

"There should be no respect between you and a deviant."[76]

Those who are aware of the Truth of Islam, believe in Allah and His Messenger ﷺ, and continue to break the laws of Islam despite this are despicable people. They should not be afforded the same respect due to others. Their words are unreliable; their testimony is not taken.

---

[75] *Jāmiʿ al-Tirmidhī*, 1921.
[76] *Al-Adab al-Mufrad*, 1018.

If you have acquaintances with such people, they should be kept at arm's length. There is no harm in returning their *salām* but they should not be considered friends and distance should be kept, lest they influence you with their poor behaviour and you find yourself becoming their peer.

2 | The Interdependent Woman

11
She Honours Her Parents

عَنْ عَائِشَةَ، قَالَتْ:

أَقْبَلَتْ فَاطِمَةُ تَمْشِي كَأَنَّ مِشْيَتَهَا مِشْيَةُ رَسُولِ اللهِ صَلَّى اللهُ عَلَيْهِ وَسَلَّمَ، فَقَالَ: مَرْحَبًا بِابْنَتِي. ثُمَّ أَجْلَسَهَا عَنْ يَمِينِهِ، أَوْ عَنْ شِمَالِهِ، ثُمَّ إِنَّهُ أَسَرَّ إِلَيْهَا حَدِيثًا، فَبَكَتْ، فَقُلْتُ لَهَا: اسْتَخَصَّكِ رَسُولُ اللهِ صَلَّى اللهُ عَلَيْهِ وَسَلَّمَ بِحَدِيثِهِ ثُمَّ تَبْكِينَ. ثُمَّ إِنَّهُ أَسَرَّ إِلَيْهَا حَدِيثًا فَضَحِكَتْ، فَقُلْتُ: مَا رَأَيْتُ كَالْيَوْمِ فَرَحًا أَقْرَبَ مِنْ حُزْنٍ، فَسَأَلْتُهَا عَمَّا قَالَ. فَقَالَتْ: مَا كُنْتُ لِأُفْشِيَ سِرَّ رَسُولِ اللهِ صَلَّى اللهُ عَلَيْهِ وَسَلَّمَ.

حَتَّى إِذَا قُبِضَ النَّبِيُّ صَلَّى اللهُ عَلَيْهِ وَسَلَّمَ سَأَلْتُهَا، فَقَالَتْ: إِنَّهُ أَسَرَّ إِلَيَّ، فَقَالَ: إِنَّ جِبْرِيلَ، عَلَيْهِ السَّلَامُ، كَانَ يُعَارِضُنِي بِالْقُرْآنِ فِي كُلِّ عَامٍ مَرَّةً، وَإِنَّهُ عَارَضَنِي بِهِ الْعَامَ مَرَّتَيْنِ، وَلَا أُرَاهُ إِلَّا قَدْ حَضَرَ أَجَلِي، وَإِنَّكِ أَوَّلُ أَهْلِ بَيْتِي لُحُوقًا بِي، وَنِعْمَ السَّلَفُ أَنَا لَكِ. فَبَكَيْتُ لِذَلِكَ، ثُمَّ قَالَ: أَلَا تَرْضَيْنَ أَنْ تَكُونِي سَيِّدَةَ نِسَاءِ هَذِهِ الْأُمَّةِ، أَوْ نِسَاءِ الْمُؤْمِنِينَ؟ قَالَتْ: فَضَحِكْتُ لِذَلِكَ.

ʿĀ'ishah narrated:

"Fāṭimah came walking; her manner of walking was akin that of Allah's Messenger ﷺ. He said, 'Welcome, my daughter.' Then he sat her on his right, or on his left, and then he whispered some words to her, and she cried. I said, 'Allah's Messenger ﷺ preferred you to receive his words and you cried?' Then he again whispered

something to her and she smiled. I said, 'I have never seen joy closer to sadness than today,' and asked her about what he said. She said, 'I will not reveal the secret of Allah's Messenger ﷺ.'

When he was taken, I asked her again, and she said, 'He confided in me, "Jibrīl ﷺ used to revise the Qur'an with me once a year, and this year he revised it with me twice. I think my time of death is near. You will be the first of my family to follow me, and what an excellent predecessor I am to you." I cried because of that, then he said, "Are you not satisfied with being the leader of the women of this nation, or the believing women?" I smiled at that.'"[77]

Filial piety is an essential characteristic of the Muslim man and woman alike. Caring for the parents that cared for you, looking after them, treating them well – these are necessary kindnesses by which we as their children should cherish them, even as they cherished us in our childhood. They gave us love, security, and essentially served us at a time when we had no power to even ask for their help. As adults, we Muslims should give back in kind and even excel in doing so. For though there is no way to fully compensate them for their love and caring, we can at least give *something* back. This is the duty of a Muslim, not merely something praiseworthy to do.

A daughter should be exemplary in her love and respect for her parents. Take the example of Sayyidah Fāṭimah ﷺ, the beloved daughter of the Prophet ﷺ, whose love for him was so great that her mannerisms became indistinguishable from those of her noble father ﷺ. Umm al-Mu'minīn Sayyidah 'Ā'ishah ﷺ narrates:

مَا رَأَيْتُ أَحَدًا كَانَ أَشْبَهَ سَمْتًا وَهَدْيًا وَدَلًّا بِرَسُولِ اللَّهِ صَلَّى اللَّهُ عَلَيْهِ وَسَلَّمَ مِنْ فَاطِمَةَ كَرَّمَ اللَّهُ وَجْهَهَا كَانَتْ إِذَا دَخَلَتْ عَلَيْهِ قَامَ إِلَيْهَا فَأَخَذَ بِيَدِهَا وَقَبَّلَهَا وَأَجْلَسَهَا فِي مَجْلِسِهِ وَكَانَ إِذَا دَخَلَ عَلَيْهَا قَامَتْ إِلَيْهِ فَأَخَذَتْ بِيَدِهِ فَقَبَّلَتْهُ وَأَجْلَسَتْهُ فِي مَجْلِسِهَا

"I have seen no one more closely resemble the disposition, mannerisms, and characteristics of Allah's Messenger ﷺ than his

---

[77] *Musnad al-Imām Aḥmad,* 26413.

daughter Fāṭimah, may Allah ennoble her countenance. If she entered his home, he would stand for her, take her by the hand, kiss her, and seat her in his place; if he entered her home, she would stand for him, take him by the hand, kiss him, and seat him in her place.[78]

Sayyidah Fāṭimah ؇ treated him exactly as he treated her, with love, kindness, and honour. A daughter should honour her parents and show them the respect they deserve. Daughters do not have the luxury of always being in the company of their parents, as they will one day, *in shā Allāh*, marry and move to the households of their husbands. A daughter should thus make great effort in honouring them whenever she is able. Our time in this world is limited, and our time with our parents is of great value. A good daughter helps with and carries out her mother's duties, and as Sayyidah Fāṭimah ؇ exemplifies, shows great love and honour for her father in every action she does. She takes his advice, understanding that a father's advice will always be sincerely given; she follows his orders, as is his right as her father; and she refrains from arguing with him. In truth, a woman should generally refrain from argumentation for argument's sake, regardless of who she is speaking to, but she should be doubly careful to avoid arguing with her father. Of course, the greatest act of filial piety is to worship Allah and as a worshipful daughter becomes a means of reward for one's parents also, but this does not preclude her from showing her parents affection and love.

Should a parent's views on a matter oppose her own, she should try to defer to their opinion, or at the very least compromise with them. Only in the matter of faith should a Muslimah oppose her parents, and even then, this opposition should be respectful. Sayyidah Asmā' bint Abū Bakr ؇ narrated:

---

[78] *Sunan Abī Dāwūd*, 5217.

أَتَتْنِي أُمِّي رَاغِبَةً، وَهْيَ مُشْرِكَةٌ، فِي عَهْدِ النَّبِيِّ صَلَّى اللَّهُ عَلَيْهِ وَسَلَّمَ، فَسَأَلْتُ النَّبِيَّ صَلَّى اللَّهُ عَلَيْهِ وَسَلَّمَ: آصِلُهَا؟ قَالَ: نَعَمْ، فَأَنْزَلَ اللَّهُ تَعَالَى فِيهَا:

لَا يَنْهَاكُمُ اللَّهُ عَنِ الَّذِينَ لَمْ يُقَاتِلُوكُمْ فِي الدِّينِ

"My mother, who was an idolater, came to me hoping for good treatment during the truce of the Prophet ﷺ, so I asked him, 'Shall I keep good relations with her?' The Prophet ﷺ said, 'Yes.' Then Allah Almighty revealed, 'Allah does not forbid you from those who do not fight you in religion'[79] regarding this matter."[80]

[79] Qur'an, 60:8.

[80] *Ṣaḥīḥ al-Bukhārī*, 2620, 5978; *Ṣaḥīḥ Muslim*, 1003.

12
She is Light-Hearted

عَنْ عَائِشَةَ رَضِـيَ اللَّهُ عَنْهَا، أَنَّهَا كَانَتْ مَعَ النَّبِيِّ صَلَّى اللَّهُ عَلَيْهِ وَسَلَّمَ فِي سَفَرٍ قَالَتْ:
فَسَابَقْتُهُ فَسَبَقْتُهُ عَلَى رِجْلَيَّ، فَلَمَّا حَمَلْتُ اللَّحْمَ سَابَقْتُهُ فَسَبَقَنِي، فَقَالَ: هَذِهِ بِتِلْكَ السَّبْقَةِ.

ʿĀ'ishah ﵂ narrated that she was with the Prophet ﷺ while on a journey, and said:

"I raced him on foot and I outran him, but when I gained some weight, I raced him again and he outran me. He said, 'This is in lieu of that race.'"[81]

Another praiseworthy quality within a woman is her positivity and light-hearted nature. Men (meaning real, masculine men) are by their nature sombre folk, their chief concerns often tied to bringing wealth to the family, protecting the household, and ensuring the spiritual and physical safety of its members. The pressure this creates within them means they are often given to melancholy and low moods. Here, a woman, whether she is a daughter, sister, wife, or mother to the man in question, can play a key role in relieving the stress and tension that the men in her life are going through by being that breath of positivity and light-heartedness that men find themselves often lacking in.

Men and women were made differently to complement one another, not to fulfil the same roles. Each gender depends on the strengths of the other to counterbalance the weaknesses found within themselves. Women seek comfort in the strength and leadership of men; men seek comfort in the softness and support of women. Across all societies, throughout history, this has always been the case. The recent move away from this normative behaviour in the Western world should not be seen as a positive evolution but a sickness that has been rejected everywhere else in the globe. Our departure from normative

---

[81] *Sunan Abī Dāwūd*, 2578.

masculine and feminine behaviours is a cause for concern, not celebration.

In the above hadith, Umm al-Mu'minīn Sayyidah ʿĀ'ishah ﵂ engaged in playful acts with her spouse, the noble Messenger of Allah ﷺ, racing him home on foot. Men are unlikely to engage in such pursuits on their own, especially men such as the Prophet ﷺ, who was the height of masculinity and the font of knowledge and spirituality in this world. But Umm al-Mu'minīn Sayyidah ʿĀ'ishah ﵂ brought out a playfulness in him. This ability to unlock the playful side of men is a gift that Allah has given women and it should be treated as such and shared with one's loved ones. With that being said, care should be taken to ensure we remain within our limits, even when engaging in fun and relaxation with our families. Umm al-Mu'minīn Sayyidah ʿĀ'ishah ﵂ narrated:

مَا رَأَيْتُ رَسُولَ اللهِ صَلَّى اللَّهُ عَلَيْهِ وَسَلَّمَ ضَاحِكًا حَتَّى أَرَى مِنْهُ لَهَوَاتِهِ إِنَّمَا كَانَ يَتَبَسَّمُ

"I never saw Allah's Messenger ﷺ laugh so much that I could see the back of his throat. Rather, he would smile."[82]

It was not the practice of the Prophet ﷺ to laugh aloud, and he never laughed excessively. Islam allows for fun, relaxation, and building family ties, but not to excess. This is especially important for womenfolk, for their voices themselves are an ʿ*awrah*[83] and thus a woman should have a care for how loudly she laughs, lest her voice carry to the ears of an unrelated man.

It should be noted here that the above does not mean that a woman should not speak in public, but that she should be aware of *how* she speaks, as her voice itself can be attractive to men. She should therefore refrain from speaking overly softly, or from giggling or drawing unnecessary attention to herself in front of unrelated men.

---

[82] *Ṣaḥīḥ al-Bukhārī*, 4551; *Ṣaḥīḥ Muslim*, 899.
[83] Something which should be guarded and protected for the sake of modesty.

13
She Embodies Sisterhood

عَنْ عَائِشَةَ - رضى الله عنها - زَوْجِ النَّبِيِّ صلى الله عليه وسلم:

... وَكَانَ رَسُولُ اللَّهِ صلى الله عليه وسلم يَسْأَلُ زَيْنَبَ بِنْتَ جَحْشٍ عَنْ أَمْرِي، فَقَالَ: يَا زَيْنَبُ، مَا عَلِمْتِ مَا رَأَيْتِ.

فَقَالَتْ: يَا رَسُولَ اللَّهِ، أَحْمِي سَمْعِي وَبَصَرِي، وَاللَّهِ مَا عَلِمْتُ عَلَيْهَا إِلاَّ خَيْرًا.

قَالَتْ: وَهْىَ الَّتِي كَانَتْ تُسَامِينِي، فَعَصَمَهَا اللَّهُ بِالْوَرَعِ.

ʿĀ'ishah ﷺ, the wife of the Prophet ﷺ, narrated:

"...Allah's Messenger ﷺ asked Zaynab bint Jaḥsh about me, saying, 'Zaynab, what do you know and what have you seen?' She replied, 'O Allah's Messenger, I refrain from claiming to hear or see what I have not. By Allah, I know nothing of her except goodness.' She said this, despite competing with me,[84] for Allah protected her with piety."[85]

Sisterhood is among the noblest qualities a Muslimah can exhibit in her daily life. Love and care for one's fellow woman, underpinned by Islamic morals and behaviour, are the foundations for a strong and flourishing Islamic society in which our children can grow into fully developed young men and women in their own right.

The bond of sisters cannot be replaced by any other relationship; a sister wishes only well for her sibling and will trust her implicitly. This is the bond of blood. Yet, the bond of creed that Islam has brought is stronger still. For though a woman can be your sister in blood, she may not share with you the single most important aspect of your life: your beliefs. Islam creates deeper bonds between women, and these bonds

---

[84] As wives of the Prophet ﷺ, they were in competition in both their beauty and the love of the Prophet ﷺ. This should not be interpreted as 'rivalry', for they had great love for one another, as can be seen here.

[85] *Ṣaḥīḥ al-Bukhārī*, 2661; *Ṣaḥīḥ Muslim*, 2770.

are every bit as strong as (and in some cases even stronger than) the bonds of blood.

The above hadith, which is a small extract from a much longer narration, is a perfect example of this. Umm al-Mu'minīn Sayyidah Zaynab bint Jaḥsh ﵂ was asked by her noble husband ﷺ with regard to Umm al-Mu'minīn Sayyidah 'Ā'ishah bint Abū Bakr ﵂, during a time when the latter's social position was being attacked. Both women were married to the same blessed man ﷺ and were thus in competition for his love, and the former had the opportunity here to take advantage of the situation and turn it in her favour. But these were no ordinary women, and their husband ﷺ was the greatest man. They had been chosen from amongst all the women in history to be his wives, and thus they embodied the perfect morals of Islam.

Umm al-Mu'minīn Sayyidah Zaynab ﵂ exhibited true sisterhood; not only did she not take advantage of the situation, but she did not choose silence here either. On the contrary, she highlighted that she would speak only the truth and then lent her support to her sister in Islam, stating what the Prophet ﷺ already knew: that there was nothing but goodness in Umm al-Mu'minīn Sayyidah 'Ā'ishah ﵂, and she was innocent of any accusations levelled against her. This is what it means to be a sister to someone: supporting another woman, despite being in competition with her, and ensuring that slander against her is swiftly done away with. It should be noted that this was not blind support, and she did not say anything that was untrue. Islam does not advocate for undeserved support, nor does it advocate for favouritism at the expense of what is right.

Sisterhood is love for another woman for the sake of Allah. It is His pleasure that is sought, not the favour of the one to whom you show sisterly care. Allah's Messenger ﷺ said,

إِنَّ اللهَ يَقُولُ يَوْمَ الْقِيَامَةِ: أَيْنَ الْمُتَحَابُّونَ بِجَلَالِي؟ الْيَوْمَ أُظِلُّهُمْ فِي ظِلِّي يَوْمَ لَا ظِلَّ إِلَّا ظِلِّي.

"Indeed, Allah will say on the Day of Resurrection, 'Where are those who have mutual love for My Glory's sake? Today I shall shelter them in My shade, a Day when there is no other shade but Mine.'"[86]

May Allah shelter all those men and women who hold mutual love and care in their hearts for their brothers and sisters for the Glory of Allah alone. *Āmīn.*

The quality of sisterhood is that of cooperation and helpfulness, enablement and encouragement. It is a noble quality, intrinsically feminine, and highlights the great favour that Allah has bestowed upon the Muslimah: that she can do great things by doing what is natural to her, and in doing so, reap greater rewards in the Hereafter. Umm al-Mu'minīn Sayyidah 'Ā'ishah bint Abū Bakr ﵄ narrated a lengthy hadith regarding the first revelation of the Qur'an. The story is well-known and does not need repeating here, however for our purposes it is worth noting the actions of Umm al-Mu'minīn Sayyidah Khadījah bint Khuwaylid ﵄, the first wife of the Prophet ﷺ and the first to accept his Prophethood and Islam.[87] She narrates:

...فَرَجَعَ بِهَا رَسُولُ اللَّهِ صلى الله عليه وسلم يَرْجُفُ فُؤَادُهُ، فَدَخَلَ عَلَى خَدِيجَةَ بِنْتِ خُوَيْلِدٍ رضى الله عنها، فَقَالَ: زَمِّلُونِي زَمِّلُونِي. فَزَمَّلُوهُ حَتَّى ذَهَبَ عَنْهُ الرَّوْعُ، فَقَالَ لِخَدِيجَةَ وَأَخْبَرَهَا الْخَبَرَ: لَقَدْ خَشِيتُ عَلَى نَفْسِي. فَقَالَتْ خَدِيجَةُ: كَلاَّ وَاللَّهِ مَا يُخْزِيكَ اللَّهُ أَبَدًا، إِنَّكَ لَتَصِلُ الرَّحِمَ، وَتَحْمِلُ الْكَلَّ، وَتَكْسِبُ الْمَعْدُومَ، وَتَقْرِي الضَّيْفَ، وَتُعِينُ عَلَى نَوَائِبِ الْحَقِّ. فَانْطَلَقَتْ بِهِ خَدِيجَةُ حَتَّى أَتَتْ بِهِ وَرَقَةَ بْنَ نَوْفَلِ بْنِ أَسَدِ بْنِ عَبْدِ الْعُزَّى ابْنَ عَمِّ خَدِيجَةَ - وَكَانَ امْرَأً تَنَصَّرَ فِي الْجَاهِلِيَّةِ، وَكَانَ يَكْتُبُ الْكِتَابَ الْعِبْرَانِيَّ، فَيَكْتُبُ مِنَ الإِنْجِيلِ بِالْعِبْرَانِيَّةِ مَا شَاءَ اللَّهُ أَنْ يَكْتُبَ، وَكَانَ شَيْخًا كَبِيرًا قَدْ عَمِيَ - فَقَالَتْ لَهُ خَدِيجَةُ: يَا ابْنَ عَمِّ اسْمَعْ مِنَ ابْنِ أَخِيكَ.

"...then Allah's Messenger ﷺ returned with the Revelation, his heart beating severely. He went to Khadījah bint Khuwaylid ﵄ and

[86] *Ṣaḥīḥ Muslim*, 2566.

[87] Again, it should be noted that Umm al-Mu'minīn Sayyidah 'Ā'ishah ﵄ is highlighting these qualities of another wife of the Prophet ﷺ, without any sort of jealousy. She highlights the noble qualities of her sister as a matter of fact.

said, *'Cover me! Cover me!'* She covered him until the awe had left him and, after that he told her what had occurred. He said, *'I fear that something may happen to me.'* Khadījah replied, *'Never! By Allah, Allah will never disgrace you. You keep good relations with your kith and kin, help the poor and the destitute, serve your guests generously, and assist the deserving afflicted ones.'* Khadījah then accompanied him to her cousin Waraqah ibn Nawfal ibn Asad ibn ʿAbd al-ʿUzzā, who had become Christian during the Age of Ignorance and wrote in Hebrew. He would write from the Gospel in Hebrew as Allah wished him to write. He was old and had lost his eyesight. Khadījah said to Waraqah, *'O cousin, listen to your nephew.'*[88]

Sisterhood and the qualities of the exemplary Muslim sister are not restricted to benefitting other women; these are qualities that are inherent within the noble woman, expressed in her every word and action. We see this in the case of Umm al-Muʾminīn Sayyidah Khadījah bint Khuwaylid ※, who exhibited these qualities perfectly. She showed great compassion to her noble husband ※, caring for him and covering him when he required it, encouraging him and highlighting his noble qualities to remind him that he had always been favoured by Allah with piety and good action. She enabled and encouraged him to seek out a person of knowledge to help confirm what he knew—that he was a Prophet and Messenger of Allah ※ and a great task had been given to him to complete.

This is what sisterhood means—to raise others up, to help them when they are down, to stand with them come what may, and ensure that they always know that they are both supported and loved.

> *...Then joining hands to little hands*
>
> *Would bid them cling together,*
>
> *"For there is no friend like a sister*

---

[88] *Ṣaḥīḥ al-Bukhārī*, 3.

In calm or stormy weather;

To cheer one on the tedious way,

To fetch one if one goes astray,

To lift one if one totters down,

To strengthen whilst one stands.[89]

[89] Christina Rosetti, The *Goblin Market.*

14
She is a Wife

عَنْ أَبِي هُرَيْرَةَ قَالَ: قَالَ رَسُولُ اللهِ صَلَّى اللَّهُ عَلَيْهِ وَسَلَّمَ:

إِذَا صَلَّتِ الْمَرْأَةُ خَمْسَهَا وَصَامَتْ شَهْرَهَا وَحَصَّنَتْ فَرْجَهَا وَأَطَاعَتْ بَعْلَهَا دَخَلَتْ مِنْ أَيِّ أَبْوَابِ الْجَنَّةِ شَاءَتْ

Abū Hurayrah narrated that Allah's Messenger ﷺ said:

"If a woman prays her five prayers, fasts her month of Ramadan, guards her chastity, and obeys her husband, she will enter Paradise from any gate she wishes."[90]

How easy Islam is to follow and how simple and perfect a religion it is! Allah's Messenger ﷺ has detailed the steps to a woman's ultimate success in a single sentence. There is no requirement to attend the mosque at all times of the day, no requirement to take up arms against the enemy in the field of war, and no requirement to go out into the world and earn a living. She need only do her compulsory acts of worship in the comfort of her home, protect herself from engaging in indecency, and obey her spouse, and every gate of Paradise will be opened for her.

Guarding one's chastity is not merely the requirement to refrain from engaging in flirtation or fornication, but anything that could lead to it, or allow others to believe it may happen or have happened. For example, Sayyidunā ʿAmr ibn al-ʿĀs narrates:

نَهَانَا رَسُولُ اللهِ صَلَّى اللهُ عَلَيْهِ وَسَلَّمَ أَنْ نَسْتَأْذِنَ عَلَى النِّسَاءِ إِلَّا بِإِذْنِ أَزْوَاجِهِنَّ

"Allah's Messenger ﷺ prohibited us from requesting entrance into women's homes without the permission of their husbands."[91]

There should be no doubt raised in the minds of others with regard to one's chastity and the utmost care should be taken to ensure this.

---

[90] *Ṣaḥīḥ Ibn Ḥibbān*, 4163.

[91] *Musnad al-Imām Aḥmad*, 17767.

Chastity and obedience to one's spouse, coupled with the fundamentals of the religion are your keys to Paradise and should be treated as such.

If one was to take no other lesson from this section, it would suffice to understand that in the obedience of one's husband lies the freedom that the modern woman so often seeks but never finds. Obedience has become a dirty word in western society, and women will often raise their noses at such a concept, taking secular liberal and feminist ideas of what it means to be a woman, and turning away from what Islam established as the best way of life for all people, regardless of gender, culture, race, or temporospatial position. Islam is *based* on obedience. Obedience to Allah, obedience to the orders of the Prophet ﷺ, and to the laws of the Sharia.

When the Prophet ﷺ is telling women to obey their husbands, why is it that women take the words of modern-day western philosophers and their agendas over his? Do we take the universally-applicable words of the one we know to be the literal Messenger ﷺ of our Creator, or do we take the words of the promiscuous, extreme feminist so-called philosophers, whose views are so fringe that they have never occurred to anyone in history, nor even anywhere else in the world in the modern age? Is having a womb our only criteria for acceptable philosophies of living?

A woman can either obey her husband (and in so doing obey Allah and His Messenger ﷺ), obey her supervisor at work, or obey her own desires. One way or another, each of us obeys someone or something. Our beloved Messenger ﷺ has asked you to obey your husband. Is this not enough for you? Allah Himself has said:

ٱلرِّجَالُ قَوَّٰمُونَ عَلَى ٱلنِّسَآءِ بِمَا فَضَّلَ ٱللَّهُ بَعْضَهُمْ عَلَىٰ بَعْضٍ وَبِمَآ أَنفَقُوا۟ مِنْ أَمْوَٰلِهِمْ ۚ
فَٱلصَّٰلِحَٰتُ قَٰنِتَٰتٌ حَٰفِظَٰتٌ لِّلْغَيْبِ بِمَا حَفِظَ ٱللَّهُ ۚ

"Men are the caretakers of women, as men have been provisioned by Allah over women and tasked with supporting them financially.

And righteous women are devoutly obedient and, when alone, protective of what Allah has entrusted them with."[92]

With that said, before a woman can obey her spouse, she has a choice to make. Islam has not come to tell women to marry whoever is decided for them and 'obey' this decision. A woman does have options and choices she can make about her own life. Of these, there is perhaps no greater choice that a woman will make in her life than choosing the one she marries. She is choosing the man who will support her and look after her, lead her and teach her, and be her constant companion in this life and the next. She is choosing the man that she will obey (so long as that obedience does not come at odds with the commands of Allah and His Messenger ﷺ), and this choice is thus more important for a woman than it is for a man. She *must* choose wisely. It should not primarily be made for wealth or for looks, nor for status or familial expectations, but for who will better her life in this world and the next through Islam. The other aspects will of course play a factor, as Islam does not require Muslims to not be *human*, but the primary reason must always be his adherence to and knowledge of the faith, for ignoring this quality will spell the downfall of not only the woman, but the progeny that follow her.

Sayyidah Fāṭimah bint Qays رضي الله عنها narrated that:

إِنَّ زَوْجَهَا طَلَّقَهَا ثَلَاثًا فَلَمْ يَجْعَلْ لَهَا رَسُولُ اللَّهِ صَلَّى اللَّهُ عَلَيْهِ وَسَلَّمَ سُكْنَى وَلَا نَفَقَةً. قَالَتْ: قَالَ لِي رَسُولُ اللَّهِ صَلَّى اللَّهُ عَلَيْهِ وَسَلَّمَ: إِذَا حَلَلْتِ فَآذِنِينِي فَآذَنْتُهُ فَخَطَبَهَا مُعَاوِيَةُ وَأَبُو جَهْمٍ وَأُسَامَةُ بْنُ زَيْدٍ، فَقَالَ رَسُولُ اللَّهِ صَلَّى اللَّهُ عَلَيْهِ وَسَلَّمَ: أَمَّا مُعَاوِيَةُ فَرَجُلٌ تَرِبٌ لَا مَالَ لَهُ وَأَمَّا أَبُو جَهْمٍ فَرَجُلٌ ضَرَّابٌ لِلنِّسَاءِ وَلَكِنْ أُسَامَةُ بْنُ زَيْدٍ. فَقَالَتْ بِيَدِهَا هَكَذَا أُسَامَةُ أُسَامَةُ. فَقَالَ لَهَا رَسُولُ اللَّهِ صَلَّى اللَّهُ عَلَيْهِ وَسَلَّمَ: طَاعَةُ اللَّهِ وَطَاعَةُ رَسُولِهِ خَيْرٌ لَكِ، قَالَتْ: فَتَزَوَّجْتُهُ فَاغْتَبَطْتُ.

Her husband had divorced her three times and Allah's Messenger ﷺ had not appointed her housing or maintenance. She said, "Allah's Messenger ﷺ said to me, 'When your waiting period is over, come to me.'" When Fāṭimah came to him, she was presented with marriage

[92] Qur'an, 4:34.

proposals from Muʿāwiyah, Abū Jahm, and Usāmah ibn Zayd. Allah's Messenger ﷺ said, "As for Muʿāwiyah, he is poor and is without property; as for Abū Jahm, he often beats women. Rather, choose Usāmah ibn Zayd." Fāṭimah indicated with her hand that she did not want Usāmah. Allah's Messenger ﷺ said, "Obedience to Allah and His Messenger is better for you."

Fāṭimah reported, "I married him and I was envied."[93]

Again, obedience to Allah and His Messenger ﷺ is key to making the correct decision. It is not for a woman to choose someone solely for their religion in isolation; after all, all of the Ṣaḥābah ﷺ were exemplary in their religion and their faith, and had this been the case then the first proposal would have been instantly acceptable. Rather, she should ensure that the candidate's religion is first sound, and then look at other factors. Can he support her, is he given to tempers and violent outbursts, will he look after, is he the father she wants her children to have? All these questions must be answered. Sayyidah Fāṭimah ﷺ chose to follow the recommendations of the Prophet ﷺ and she was rewarded for that obedience with a great man with whom to spend her days in this life and the next.

[93] *Ṣaḥīḥ Muslim*, 1480.

15
She is Ever Loyal and Dutiful

عَنْ عَائِشَةَ ـ رضى الله عنها ـ قَالَتْ:

قَالَ رَسُولُ اللَّهِ صلى الله عليه وسلم: إِنِّي لأَعْرِفُ غَضَبَكِ وَرِضَاكِ. قَالَتْ، قُلْتُ: وَكَيْفَ تَعْرِفُ ذَاكَ يَا رَسُولَ اللَّهِ؟ قَالَ: إِنَّكِ إِذَا كُنْتِ رَاضِيَةً قُلْتِ بَلَى وَرَبِّ مُحَمَّدٍ. وَإِذَا كُنْتِ سَاخِطَةً قُلْتِ لاَ وَرَبِّ إِبْرَاهِيمَ. قَالَتْ، قُلْتُ: أَجَلْ لَسْتُ أُهَاجِرُ إِلاَّ اسْمَكَ.

ʿĀ'ishah ﵂ narrates:

"Allah's Messenger ﷺ said, 'I know when you are angry and when you are pleased.' I said, 'And how do you know that, O Allah's Messenger?' He said, 'When you are pleased, you say, "Of course, by the Lord of Muhammad," but when you are angry you say, "No, by the Lord of Ibrāhīm!"' I said, 'Indeed! I leave nothing out except your name.'"[94]

Loyalty and duty to one's spouse should be absolute. Whether we are in a state of happiness, sorrow, or anger, our duties do not change. A Muslimah always has these two qualities of dutifulness to her husband and complete loyalty to him. Above, we see that Umm al-Mu'minīn Sayyidah ʿĀ'ishah ﵂, regardless of her mood or emotional state, remained ever respectful to her noble husband ﷺ. The only difference in the way that she spoke to him was in how she referenced Allah in the conversation. No thought of churlishness, disrespect, or insubordination even crossed her mind. In a similar narration, the Prophet ﷺ pointed out another sign that would indicate when Umm al-Mu'minīn Sayyidah ʿĀ'ishah ﵂ was upset. She narrates that Allah's Messenger ﷺ said:

[94] *Ṣaḥīḥ al-Bukhārī*, 6078.

إِذَا غَضِبْتِ قُلْتِ: يَا مُحَمَّدُ، وَإِذَا رَضِيتِ قُلْتِ: يَا رَسُولَ اللهِ

"When you are upset you say, 'O Muhammad', and when you are pleased you say, 'O Allah's Messenger!'"[95]

Even when one is angry with one's husband, these qualities can and should still be present within you. Respect and obedience of your husband should not be contingent upon your mood. The respect of Umm al-Mu'minīn Sayyidah ʿĀ'ishah ﷺ for her noble husband ﷺ was ever clear; whether emotional or angry, she would never be insubordinate to him. It is also plain to see that there was an element of playfulness in their relationship, as can be seen from the teasing of the Prophet ﷺ. Umm al-Mu'minīn Sayyidah ʿĀ'ishah ﷺ narrates:

كُنْتُ أَغْتَسِلُ أَنَا وَرَسُولُ اللهِ صَلَّى اللهُ عَلَيْهِ وَسَلَّمَ مِنْ إِنَاءٍ وَاحِدٍ مِنَ الْجَنَابَةِ.

"Allah's Messenger ﷺ and I used to wash from the same vessel[96] *for ritual impurity."*[97]

This is how a marriage should be. There was a clear hierarchy in the household, with respect and obedience being afforded to her noble husband ﷺ, and there was mutual love and affection between them both. Their household was not a sombre one, but was full of joy and happiness. Yet, as we read in the tenth hadith in this book, the household's hierarchy should always be clear. Sayyidunā Abū Hurayrah ﷺ narrated that the Prophet ﷺ said,

لَوْ كُنْتُ آمِرًا أَحَدًا أَنْ يَسْجُدَ لأَحَدٍ لأَمَرْتُ الْمَرْأَةَ أَنْ تَسْجُدَ لِزَوْجِهَا.

---

[95] *Musnad al-Imām Aḥmad,* 24010.

[96] This narration should not be taken as an excuse for spouses to shower together unclothed. Islamic etiquette and decency dictate that even when engaged in intimacy spouses should remain clothed to some degree. Here, 'bathing' means *ghusl,* and this can be done whilst clothed. The high morals of the Prophet ﷺ would not allow him to be fully unclothed, even in front of his wife.

[97] *Musnad al-Imām Aḥmad,* 24014.

"Were I to order anyone to prostrate to another, I would order the wife to prostrate to her husband."[98]

As mentioned previously, this hadith is not advocating for prostration, but using a hypothetical situation to show the level of devotedness, loyalty, commitment, and dutifulness that a woman should have for her husband. She should maintain ties with those whom he maintains ties with, and protect herself from any situation where it could lead to his displeasure. This is to the extent that Sayyidunā Abū Saʿīd ﵁ narrates:

نَهَى رَسُولُ اللهِ صَلَّى اللهُ عَلَيْهِ وَسَلَّمَ النِّسَاءَ أَنْ يَصُمْنَ إِلَّا بِإِذْنِ أَزْوَاجِهِنَّ

"Allah's Messenger ﷺ prohibited wives from fasting without their husbands' permission."[99]

This is because if she is fasting, she may not be able to carry out the duties that her husband requires of her. Of course, this is only in relation to supererogatory fasting, as obedience to the commandments of Allah far outweighs obedience to any human being.

All of this is to say that a married woman should focus on perfecting these characteristics and others within herself. She must be dutiful and committed to the happiness of her spouse, as this will be a means for her to enter Paradise. But she must also embody the qualities of passivity and surrender with her husband, for no real man is attracted to a woman who is assertive and seeks to dominate him. To be non-forceful in your dealings with him, to be shy and receptive to him, to rely on him and depend upon him – these are qualities which will push his masculinity to the fore and make him feel and become more manly and protective of you as a result, which will in turn make you feel more feminine and comfortable in your womanhood.

A woman should be willing to give herself completely to her husband, emotionally, mentally, and physically, and seek to please

---

[98] *Jāmiʿ al-Tirmidhī*, 1159.
[99] *Sunan Ibn Mājah*, 1762.

him. She offers him comfort, love, and happiness in exchange for his protection, guidance, and provision. Through this interdependence, the conditional love of newlyweds becomes the unconditional love of lifelong spouses. To do otherwise is to invite calamity. Sayyidunā Abū Hurayrah ﷺ narrates that Allah's Messenger ﷺ said,

إِذَا بَاتَتِ الْمَرْأَةُ هَاجِرَةً فِرَاشَ زَوْجِهَا لَعَنَتْهَا الْمَلاَئِكَةُ حَتَّى تُصْبِحَ.

"When a woman spends the night away from her husband's bed, the angels curse her until the morning."[100]

He ﷺ also narrates that Allah's Messenger ﷺ said,

وَالَّذِي نَفْسِي بِيَدِهِ مَا مِنْ رَجُلٍ يَدْعُو امْرَأَتَهُ إِلَى فِرَاشِهِ فَتَأْبَى عَلَيْهِ إِلَّا كَانَ الَّذِي فِي السَّمَاءِ ساخطا عَلَيْهَا حَتَّى يرضى عَنْهَا.

"By Him in Whose Hand is my soul, no woman refuses her man's calling her to his bed except that He Who is in Heaven is displeased with her until her husband is pleased with her."[101]

The happiness of your Sustainer is tied to the happiness of those through whom He sustains you; in this case, it is the husband. A woman should not only be receptive to her husband in terms of intimacy, but also actively facilitate it. It is often the case that men will initiate the act themselves, but it is not their task alone to do, and the woman too should actively seek to engage her husband in intimacy, thereby increasing the love between them. The etiquettes of Islamic life should nevertheless remain at the forefront, even within the privacy of the marital bedroom. Sayyidunā ʿUtbah ibn ʿAbd al-Sulamī ﷺ narrates that Allah's Messenger ﷺ said,

إِذَا أَتَى أَحَدُكُمْ أَهْلَهُ فَلْيَسْتَتِرْ وَلَا يَتَجَرَّدْ تَجَرُّدَ الْعَيْرَيْنِ

"When one of you comes to their spouse, let them cover themselves and not approach each other like two wild mules."[102]

[100] *Ṣaḥīḥ Muslim*, 1436a.
[101] *Ṣaḥīḥ Muslim*, 1436c.
[102] *Sunan Ibn Mājah*, 1921.

This means that even at the height of passion, even when it threatens to overwhelm, there should still always be a degree of modesty between them. They should refrain from becoming completely unclothed, and should engage in kind words, kissing, and foreplay. Marital intimacy and the closeness that it builds between two people is a blessing from Allah. As Muslims, we must be mindful not to fall into the throes of lust and forget that Allah has blessed us with both the nobility of humanity and the nobility of Islam. It is not the behaviour of a Muslim to lose all sense of decency once the bedroom door closes.

16
She is Gentle

عَنْ عَائِشَةَ قَالَتْ قَالَ رَسُولُ اللَّهِ صَلَّى اللَّهُ عَلَيْهِ وَسَلَّمَ:
إِنَّ اللَّهَ رَفِيقٌ يُحِبُّ الرِّفْقَ فِي الْأَمْرِ كُلِّهِ

ʿĀ'ishah narrated that Allah's Messenger ﷺ said:

"Indeed Allah is gentle and He loves gentleness in all matters."[108]

There are certain Godly qualities that are found in abundance in womenfolk, such as mercy, compassion, caring, kindness, and gentleness. These are qualities that Allah has been described to have, both by Himself and via the Prophet ﷺ. A true woman is sweet, but hides this sweetness from those who do not have the right to witness it. She is openly caring and merciful; in fact, the word for womb in Arabic is '*raḥim*' which is derived from Allah's own names (al-Raḥmān and al-Raḥīm) to honour the special status of a mother and the inherent mercy found within her.

Umm al-Mu'minīn Sayyidah ʿĀ'ishah ؓ narrates that the Prophet ﷺ said,

إِنَّ الرِّفْقَ لَا يَكُونُ فِي شَيْءٍ إِلَّا زَانَهُ وَلَا يُنْزَعُ مِنْ شَيْءٍ إِلَّا شَانَهُ

"Indeed gentleness is not found in anything except that it beautifies it and it is not removed from anything except that it blemishes it."[104]

This is the quality that truly beautifies women: a woman is gentle by her nature. She does not pick and choose to whom or what she shows her mercy to. Women who feel nothing for starving children elsewhere in the world, solely for the reason that they do not look like them are not true women. Muslimahs who feel nothing for the oppressed,

---

[108] *Ṣaḥīḥ al-Bukhārī*, 6927; *Ṣaḥīḥ Muslim*, 2165.
[104] *Ṣaḥīḥ Muslim*, 2594.

simply because they are not of the same race or from the same place are equally removed from true womanhood. A woman cares for all living things, feels mercy and kindness toward them, and is compassionate. Sayyidunā Abū Hurayrah ﷺ reports that the Prophet ﷺ said,

غُفِرَ لِامْرَأَةٍ مُومِسَةٍ مَرَّتْ بِكَلْبٍ عَلَى رَأْسِ رَكِيٍّ يَلْهَثُ قَالَ كَادَ يَقْتُلُهُ الْعَطَشُ فَنَزَعَتْ خُفَّهَا فَأَوْثَقَتْهُ بِخِمَارِهَا فَنَزَعَتْ لَهُ مِنْ الْمَاءِ فَغُفِرَ لَهَا بِذَلِكَ.

"A prostitute who passed by a dog panting near a well was forgiven. Thirst had nearly killed the dog, so she removed her moccasin and tied it to her muffler, and then drew some water for it. For this, Allah forgave her."[105]

Sayyidunā Abū Hurayrah ﷺ also reports that the Prophet ﷺ said,

دَخَلَتِ امْرَأَةٌ النَّارَ مِنْ جَرَّاءِ هِرَّةٍ لَهَا أَوْ هِرٍّ رَبَطَتْهَا فَلَا هِيَ أَطْعَمَتْهَا وَلَا هِيَ أَرْسَلَتْهَا تُرَمِّمُ مِنْ خَشَاشِ الْأَرْضِ حَتَّى مَاتَتْ هَزْلًا

"A woman entered the Hellfire because of a cat or kitten she had imprisoned. She neither fed it nor released it to eat the vermin of the earth until it died, emaciated."[106]

In the first hadith, a promiscuous woman, whom we would usually label as one of extremely poor character, was forgiven for all her evil actions because of the mercy she showed to a thirsty animal. The fact that she was a prostitute or that the one being shown mercy was a dog did not diminish the act in the Sight of Allah. This was an action of pure kindness, where she did not expect anything in return. She was rewarded with Allah's forgiveness. As Allah says in the Qur'an:

وَسَيُجَنَّبُهَا ٱلْأَتْقَى (١٧) ٱلَّذِى يُؤْتِى مَالَهُۥ يَتَزَكَّىٰ (١٨) وَمَا لِأَحَدٍ عِندَهُۥ مِن نِّعْمَةٍ تُجْزَىٰٓ (١٩) إِلَّا ٱبْتِغَآءَ وَجْهِ رَبِّهِ ٱلْأَعْلَىٰ (٢٠) وَلَسَوْفَ يَرْضَىٰ (٢١)

But the righteous will be spared from it (the Raging Fire) – those who donate of their wealth only to purify themselves, not in return for

---

[105] *Ṣaḥīḥ al-Bukhārī*, 3321; *Ṣaḥīḥ Muslim*, 2245.
[106] *Ṣaḥīḥ Muslim*, 2619.

someone's favours, but seeking the pleasure of their Lord, the Most High. They will certainly be pleased.[107]

On the other hand, we have the woman who went against her God-given nature and starved an animal she could have easily fed or released. Her act was one of inherent cruelty, and as such her fate was the opposite of the first's. There was no mercy to be found for the woman who had no mercy. Sayyidunā Jarīr ibn 'Abdullāh ؓ narrated that the Prophet ﷺ said,

مَنْ لاَ يَرْحَمْ لاَ يُرْحَمْ

"Whoever has no mercy, gets no mercy."[108]

Kindness to others is a prerequisite to receiving Allah's Mercy, and women have been gifted with the quality of mercy in their *fiṭrah*. They have been created with gentleness and compassion in excess. In the modern age, this quality is slowly being eroded from the psyche of womankind, as society shifts closer and closer to androgyny through attrition. It is incumbent upon us as Muslims to prevent this from occurring; this mindset must be actively fought, not merely ignored. Gentleness is a quality of Allah, which He loves, and to allow it to erode away from our own behaviour is to invite great calamity. Umm al-Mu'minīn Sayyidah 'Ā'ishah ؓ narrates that Allah's Messenger ﷺ said,

إِنَّ اللَّهَ رَفِيقٌ يُحِبُّ الرِّفْقَ وَيُعْطِي عَلَى الرِّفْقِ مَا لاَ يُعْطِي عَلَى الْعُنْفِ وَمَا لاَ يُعْطِي عَلَى مَا سِوَاهُ

"Indeed, Allah is gentle and He loves gentleness. He rewards for gentleness what is not granted for harshness, and He rewards nothing else like it."[109]

---

[107] Qur'an, 92:17-21.
[108] *Ṣaḥīḥ al-Bukhārī*, 6013.
[109] *Ṣaḥīḥ Muslim*, 2593.

17
She is Financially Responsible

عَنْ أَبِي هُرَيْرَةَ، قَالَ:

قِيلَ لِرَسُولِ اللَّهِ صلى الله عليه وسلم أَىُّ النِّسَاءِ خَيْرٌ؟ قَالَ الَّتِي تَسُرُّهُ إِذَا نَظَرَ وَتُطِيعُهُ إِذَا أَمَرَ وَلاَ تُخَالِفُهُ فِي نَفْسِهَا وَمَالِهَا بِمَا يَكْرَهُ.

Abū Hurayrah narrates:

"It was said to Allah's Messenger ﷺ, 'Which woman is best?' He replied, 'The one who pleases him when he looks at her, obeys him when he commands her, and does not go against his wishes with regard to herself nor her wealth.'"[110]

Financial responsibility and scrupulousness are qualities of the best of people, not only the best of women. However, the Prophet ﷺ mentioned these three characteristics when describing the best woman: that the sight of her gives her husband joy, that she is obedient, and that she does not go against him regarding herself and wealth. The first two characteristics are quite easily understood from the wording of the hadith itself. However, for our current purposes the last quality requires further scrutiny.

Allah says in the Qur'an:

ٱلرِّجَالُ قَوَّٰمُونَ عَلَى ٱلنِّسَآءِ بِمَا فَضَّلَ ٱللَّهُ بَعْضَهُمْ عَلَىٰ بَعْضٍ وَبِمَآ أَنفَقُوا۟ مِنْ أَمْوَٰلِهِمْ ۚ فَٱلصَّـٰلِحَـٰتُ قَـٰنِتَـٰتٌ حَـٰفِظَـٰتٌ لِّلْغَيْبِ بِمَا حَفِظَ ٱللَّهُ ۚ

"Men are the caretakers of women, as men have been provisioned by Allah over women and tasked with supporting them financially. And righteous women are devoutly obedient and, when alone, protective of what Allah has entrusted them with."[111]

Allah Himself has described the righteous woman as 'devoutly obedient' and 'protective of what Allah has entrusted them with' 'when

---

[110] Abū ʿAbd al-Raḥmān Aḥmad ibn Shuʿayb al-Nasāʾī, *Sunan al-Nasāʾī*, 3231.
[111] Qur'an, 4:34.

alone'. That a righteous woman is protective of her modesty and honour goes without saying, but the *āyah* also implies that the righteous woman is protective of the wealth she has been entrusted with. This means not spending the wealth she has access to excessively or frivolously. Every penny has a purpose, every pound is accounted for.

It is the man's responsibility to bring wealth into the household to ensure the needs of his family are met; it is the woman's responsibility to ensure the finances that he brings into the house and puts in her care go as far as possible in ensuring the long-term welfare of the household. She must work hard to invest the money only in what is required. If there is a desire or wish to spend their wealth on anything beyond what is necessary, then this must be discussed with her husband. Only after consultation and permission should the wealth be spent in this way. With that said, Umm al-Mu'minīn Sayyidah ʿĀ'ishah ﵂ narrates:

جَاءَتْ هِنْدُ بِنْتُ عُتْبَةَ بْنِ رَبِيعَةَ فَقَالَتْ: يَا رَسُولَ اللهِ إِنَّ أَبَا سُفْيَانَ رَجُلٌ مِسِّيكٌ فَهَلْ عَلَيَّ حَرَجٌ أَنْ أُطْعِمَ مِنْ الَّذِي لَهُ عِيَالَنَا؟ فَقَالَ صَلَّى اللهُ عَلَيْهِ وَسَلَّمَ: لَا حَرَجَ عَلَيْكِ أَنْ تُطْعِمِيهِمْ بِالْمَعْرُوفِ

"Hind bint ʿUtbah came and said, 'O Allah's Messenger, Abū Sufyān is a parsimonious man. Can I be blamed for using his wealth to feed our dependents?' The Prophet ﷺ said, 'There is no blame if you feed them reasonably.'"[112]

Part of a woman's financial responsibility is to ensure that her husband's dependents are looked after, clothed, and fed. So, if you require groceries to feed your children, there is no need to ask your husband's permission for this, though it is still preferable and good manners to do so and permission should always be sought in the first instance. Likewise, if your children *require* clothes,[113] or bills need paying, there is no harm in spending in these situations either.

---

[112] *Ṣaḥīḥ al-Bukhārī*, 2328; *Ṣaḥīḥ Muslim*, 1714.

[113] The word 'require' has been italicised to emphasise that this is only justifiable if it is truly required. If the children do not have enough clothes to get by, then by all means

Using finances for the long-term welfare of one's husband and his household includes spending wealth in the path of Allah. Umm al-Mu'minīn Sayyidah ʿĀ'ishah ﵂ narrates that the Prophet ﷺ said,

إِذَا أَنْفَقَتِ الْمَرْأَةُ - وَقَالَ أَبِي فِي حَدِيثِهِ إِذَا أَطْعَمَتِ الْمَرْأَةُ - مِنْ بَيْتِ زَوْجِهَا غَيْرَ مُفْسِدَةٍ كَانَ لَهَا أَجْرُهَا وَلَهُ مِثْلُهُ بِمَا اكْتَسَبَ وَلَهَا بِمَا أَنْفَقَتْ وَلِلْخَازِنِ مِثْلُ ذَلِكَ مِنْ غَيْرِ أَنْ يَنْقُصَ مِنْ أُجُورِهِمْ شَيْئًا.

"When a woman spends (or when a woman feeds the poor) from her husband's hold, without spending excessively, she will have her reward; he will be rewarded in kind for he earned it and she will be rewarded for what she spent. The same applies to the storekeeper, without detracting from their rewards."[114]

So, if a woman spends her husband's wealth in charity, all involved will share the reward for this charitable act, and such actions are encouraged – so long as she does not go into excess. Should she wish to donate a large amount, she should again ask her husband's permission first. It is for each household to decide what is a large amount for them, based on their own situation; one hundred dollars or pounds may be a week's wage for some and a day's spend for others. Sayyidah Asmā' bint Abū Bakr ﵂ narrates:

قُلْتُ: يَا رَسُولَ اللَّهِ إِنَّهُ لَيْسَ لِي مِنْ بَيْتِي إِلَّا مَا أَدْخَلَ عَلَيَّ الزُّبَيْرُ أَفَأُعْطِي؟ قَالَ: نَعَمْ وَلَا تُوكِي فَيُوكَى عَلَيْكِ.

"I asked, 'O Allah's Messenger, I have nothing in my house but what was given to me by my husband, al-Zubayr. Should I give it to charity?'

The Prophet ﷺ said, 'Yes, do not hold onto it, lest Allah hold it against you.'"[115]

---

spend on them. If you *feel* like buying them more clothes beyond their requirement, this again falls into excess.

[114] *Sunan Ibn Mājah*, 2294.

[115] *Jāmiʿ al-Tirmidhī*, 1960.

Each coin we hold onto, every bit of wealth we have with us when we die, will be accounted for by Allah. Thus, everything we have spent in His path has been invested in the betterment of our ultimate future, and everything we held back may be held as evidence against us. Take care of how you spend your wealth. Allah says:

وَٱلْعَصْرِ (١) إِنَّ ٱلْإِنسَـٰنَ لَفِى خُسْرٍ (٢) إِلَّا ٱلَّذِينَ ءَامَنُوا۟ وَعَمِلُوا۟ ٱلصَّـٰلِحَـٰتِ وَتَوَاصَوْا۟
بِٱلْحَقِّ وَتَوَاصَوْا۟ بِٱلصَّبْرِ (٣)

"By the time! Surely humanity is in loss, except those who have faith, do good, and urge each other to the truth, and urge each other to perseverance."[116]

There are only two currencies of worth. Time, which is spent whether it is used or not, is the only currency of value in this life, and should be spent well by exchanging it for the only currency of value in the Hereafter: our deeds. Invest your time in the Hereafter, for every moment spent in goodness becomes manifold profit, and every moment wasted is a manifold loss. Wealth spent in charity is never wasted.

[116] Qur'an, 103:1-3.

18
She is Motherly

عَنْ مُعَاوِيَةَ بْنِ جَاهِمَةَ السَّلَمِيِّ:

أَنَّ جَاهِمَةَ جَاءَ إِلَى النَّبِيِّ صَلَّى اللَّهُ عَلَيْهِ وَسَلَّمَ فَقَالَ: يَا رَسُولَ اللهِ، أَرَدْتُ أَنْ أَغْزُوَ وَقَدْ جِئْتُ أَسْتَشِيرُكَ. فَقَالَ: هَلْ لَكَ مِنْ أُمٍّ؟ قَالَ: نَعَمْ. قَالَ: فَالْزَمْهَا، فَإِنَّ الْجَنَّةَ تَحْتَ رِجْلَيْهَا.

Muʿāwiyah ibn Jāhimah narrated:

"Jāhimah came to the Prophet ﷺ and said, 'O Allah's Messenger, I intend to join the military expedition and have come seeking your counsel.' The Prophet ﷺ asked, 'Do you have a mother?' He replied, 'Yes.' The Prophet ﷺ said, 'Then stay with her, for Paradise lies beneath her feet.'"[117]

There is no greater honour that can be bestowed upon a woman than the honour of motherhood. It is the one thing that women can do that men can never emulate. A man can father his child through conception, and he can father him through being his parent, but he can never *mother* the child. It is indeed a great gift and honour.

A woman grows her child within her body for 9 months, protecting him and nurturing him in such a way that he does not even know that there is anything at all beyond his mother's womb. Everything he sees, hears, feels, and the very fluid he breathes – it is all her. She is his world. When he is born, she goes through great hardship and pain to help bring him into this world, and when he opens his eyes and is blinded by this entirely new realm outside of the safety of her womb, he cries out in terror and pain and anguish, only wishing to be comforted by her familiar heartbeat once more. He only settles when he is safe in her arms. She cares for him throughout the following years of his life, breastfeeding him, clothing him, and cleaning him. She teaches him language, morals, and manners. When the boy reaches manhood, their mutual love is something that the father can never

[117] *Sunan al-Nasāʾī*, 3104.

claim, for Allah has made a special place for the mother in the hearts of her children.

Sayyidunā Ibn Abi Mulaykah ﵁ narrates:

كَانَتْ فَاطِمَةُ تَنْقُزُ الْحَسَنَ بْنَ عَلِيٍّ وَتَقُولُ:

بِأَبِي شَبَهُ النَّبِيِّ ... لَيْسَ شَبِيهًا بِعَلِيِّ

"Fāṭimah used to play with al-Ḥasan ibn Alī, saying,

'My Prophet Father he resembles much,

But not his father 'Alī's face as such.'"[118]

Playing with the children of Sayyidunā 'Alī ﵁, nurturing them, and raising them up in a loving household was absolutely the most important and valuable thing that the beloved daughter of the Prophet ﷺ could do. In the time of the Ṣaḥābah ﵃ it was not even a question. Ask the modern-day 'feminist Muslimah' to name one Ṣaḥābiyah ﵂ that placed more importance on being a businesswoman than being a mother, and you will get no worthwhile response.

A mother's role in any functioning society is of great importance. No society can function or continue to exist when the family unit is broken, and no family can exist without the role of the mother being filled. We live in an age and a society where women are taught to look down at the homemaker and the stay-at-home mother, as if one's value can only be measured by their social contribution to the workforce. The *absolute importance* of mothers as the cornerstones of society seems to have been belittled and ignored until it has become all but forgotten. Tell your friend that you are a homemaker, and she will think *unemployed*; tell her you are a stay-at-home mother, and she will consider you reliant on 'working people' like herself for handouts; but if you tell her you are a nurse, a teacher, or an office worker, she will cheer you on. Such thinking is nothing but blind folly.

---

[118] *Musnad al-Imām Aḥmad*, 26422.

When the Western world tells you that being miserable at work is superior to feeling fulfilled by *doing the very thing that your mind, body, and soul are designed to do*, being deceived and believing every false word that drips from the fangs of the venomous vipers that spit out these lies. When your noble Prophet ﷺ has told you of the high status that a mother has in Islamic society, you scoff. Sayyidunā Abū Hurayrah ؓ narrated:

جَاءَ رَجُلٌ إِلَى رَسُولِ اللَّهِ صَلَّى اللَّهُ عَلَيْهِ وَسَلَّمَ فَقَالَ مَنْ أَحَقُّ النَّاسِ بِحُسْنِ صَحَابَتِي؟ قَالَ أُمُّكَ. قَالَ ثُمَّ مَنْ؟ قَالَ ثُمَّ أُمُّكَ. قَالَ ثُمَّ مَنْ؟ قَالَ ثُمَّ أُمُّكَ. قَالَ ثُمَّ مَنْ؟ قَالَ ثُمَّ أَبُوكَ.

"A man approached Allah's Messenger ﷺ and asked him, 'Who amongst the people is most deserving of my good company?' The Prophet ﷺ said, 'Your mother.' The man asked, 'Who next?' The Prophet ﷺ said, 'Your mother.' The man asked again, 'And then who?' The Prophet ﷺ again said, 'Your mother.' The man asked again, 'And then who?' The Prophet ﷺ replied, 'Your father.'"[119]

The question posed was not 'who amongst my family is more deserving' but 'who amongst the *people*'. The mother has such a high status in Islamic society that she was mentioned three times as the most deserving of good company and kind treatment. And why should this not be so, when Paradise itself lies beneath her feet?

Allah made women to fulfil this role. A good woman is motherly and tender; she nurtures her children and develops them into the future fathers and mothers of society. There is no greater role a woman can play in society than this, and yet we continue to consume lies that belittle this most vital of societal building blocks. It is to the point where we are teaching our daughters to hold off on having children of their own until they have 'achieved what they want from their careers'. Positions and accolades in the workplace will never fulfil the void you feel in the pit of your stomach, nor bring you true joy and happiness in your life. Ask the woman who cannot have children what she would

---

[119] *Ṣaḥīḥ al-Bukhārī*, 5971; *Ṣaḥīḥ Muslim*, 2548.

give to be a mother; ask the woman who had a child and lost her what she would give to have her back.

Motherhood is a position that all women should strive for if they are able to bear children. Even if they are not, they should consider adoption or fostering to fulfil the *fundamental need* they have to be mothers. It is time that we move away from the disdain and mockery that our failed societies have directed at the mother and see these women for what they are: the bastions of traditional virtue, the foundation stones of society, and the most deserving people of our love and respect.

19
She Cares

عَنْ أَبِي أُذَيْنَةَ الصَّدَفِيِّ أَنَّ رَسُولَ اللهِ صَلَّى اللهُ عَلَيْهِ وَسَلَّمَ قَالَ:

خَيْرُ نِسَائِكُمُ الْوَدُودُ الْوَلُودُ الْمُوَاتِيَةُ الْمُوَاسِيَةُ إِذَا اتَّقَيْنَ اللهَ وَشَرُّ نِسَائِكُمُ الْمُتَبَرِّجَاتُ الْمُتَخَيِّلاتُ وَهُنَّ الْمُنَافِقَاتُ لا يَدْخُلُ الْجَنَّةَ مِنْهُنَّ إِلا مِثْلُ الْغُرَابِ الأَعْصَمِ

Abū Udhaynah al-Ṣadafī narrates that Allah's Messenger ﷺ said:

"The best of your women are loving, fertile, favourable, and comforting, when they are cognisant of Allah. The worst of your women unveil their beauty, take pride in their appearance, and they are hypocrites. None of them will enter Paradise except (those who are) like the rare crow."[120]

The above hadith contains many great lessons therein, most of which are self-explanatory. Being loving, fertile, and favourable are not merely benefits for the husband, although they are definitely also that, but these qualities are beneficial for Muslim society as a whole, as the Prophet ﷺ advised,

تَزَوَّجُوا الْوَدُودَ الْوَلُودَ فَإِنِّي مُكَاثِرٌ بِكُمُ الأُمَمَ.

"Marry women who are loving and fertile, for I shall exult in your outnumbering all nations."[121]

That the worst of women, being prideful of their appearance, unveiling their beauty to the world, and being hypocritical, are also possessive of clearly low, poor qualities, is equally self-evident. The description of the Prophet ﷺ of those that have these low qualities but still enter Paradise as 'rare crows' is equally clear.

Our main focus in this section is the word '*muwāsiyah*' or 'comforting'. A woman who has this quality consoles and comforts her partner, showing empathy and understanding. These qualities are not

[120] Abū Bakr Aḥmad ibn al-Ḥusayn al-Bayhaqī, *al-Sunan al-Kubrā*, 12480.
[121] *Sunan Abī Dāwūd*, 2050.

just reserved for her husband, but to her friends and family. She cares about how others feel and works to ensure that those who are upset feel cared for and looked after.

All cultures throughout the ages have placed great stock in women who portray the qualities of sensitivity, emotion, and passion as, like many of the traits and characteristics we have covered thus far, they are almost uniquely feminine. Women find it much easier than men to show empathy to others, likely due to their core natural and social function of motherhood, and they are thus well-suited to the role of comforter and carer. A perfect example of this has already been given earlier with the narration about how Umm al-Mu'minīn Khadijah ﵁ comforted the Prophet ﷺ when he first received revelation. Women empathise with others, try their best to understand what their counterpart is feeling, and then offer them comfort. Where a masculine response to problems would be to provide solutions, a feminine response is to provide support. Men focus on the problem; women focus on the person.

Women are emotional, sensitive beings by their nature, and thus the best of them are passionate. They are passionate about people and about helping them; they are passionate and empathetic by their very nature. When they see someone going through hardship, they feel what the other is feeling. When someone is struggling, they understand the struggle.

This natural empathy should also extend to an aversion to vengefulness and causing other people harm. The worst women are those who have no empathy and take joy from harm inflicted on others. By extension, the best are those who hate to see others be harmed, regardless of who they are. Sayyidunā Nāfiʿ ﵀ narrates:

لَقِيَ ابْنُ عُمَرَ ابْنَ صَائِدٍ فِي بَعْضِ طُرُقِ الْمَدِينَةِ، فَقَالَ لَهُ قَوْلاً أَغْضَبَهُ فَانْتَفَخَ حَتَّى مَلأَ السِّكَّةَ، فَدَخَلَ ابْنُ عُمَرَ عَلَى حَفْصَةَ وَقَدْ بَلَغَهَا فَقَالَتْ لَهُ: رَحِمَكَ اللَّهُ مَا أَرَدْتَ مِنِ ابْنِ صَائِدٍ؟ أَمَا عَلِمْتَ أَنَّ رَسُولَ اللَّهِ صلى الله عليه وسلم قَالَ: إِنَّمَا يَخْرُجُ مِنْ غَضْبَةٍ يَغْضَبُهَا؟

"'Abdullāh ibn 'Umar met Ibn Ṣā'id[122] *on one of the paths of Madinah and said to him a word which enraged him. He became so swollen with anger that the way was blocked. Ibn 'Umar went to Ḥafṣah and informed her about this. Thereupon she said, 'May Allah have mercy upon you, why did you incite Ibn Ṣā'id? Do you not know that Allah's Messenger ﷺ warned, "It will be the extreme rage that will draw out (the Dajjāl)"?'"*[123]

In another narration, Sayyidunā 'Abdullāh ibn 'Umar ﷺ is described as reacting to Ibn Ṣā'id's anger by striking him so hard with his staff that it broke. In that narration, Umm al-Mu'minīn Sayyidah Ḥafṣah bint Umar ﷺ said,

مَا شَأْنُكَ وَشَأْنُهُ؟ مَا يُولِعُكَ بِهِ؟ أَمَا سَمِعْتَ رَسُولَ اللهِ صَلَّى اللهُ عَلَيْهِ وَسَلَّمَ يَقُولُ:
إِنَّمَا يَخْرُجُ الدَّجَّالُ مِنْ غَضْبَةٍ يَغْضَبُهَا

"What is wrong with the two of you? What do you seek from him, when you have heard Allah's Messenger ﷺ saying, 'The Dajjāl will come out due to the extreme rage he feels'?"[124]

Umm al-Mu'minīn Sayyidah Ḥafṣah bint 'Umar ﷺ highlighted the sayings of the Noble Prophet ﷺ to remind Sayyidunā 'Abdullāh ibn 'Umar ﷺ of the consequences of anger. The very existence of anger itself is a cause for future calamities. A good woman is a calming presence for the men in her life and constantly reminds them to control their anger. Umm al-Mu'minīn Sayyidah Ḥafṣah bint Umar ﷺ herself narrates that the Prophet of Allah ﷺ said,

إِنَّ أَوَّلَ مَا يَبْعَثُهُ اللهُ عَلَى النَّاسِ غَضْبَةً يَغْضَبُهَا

"The first thing that Allah will send upon the people is rage."[125]

---

[122] It is said that Ibn Ṣā'id was one of the minor Dajjāls, although he himself vehemently denied this.

[123] *Ṣaḥīḥ Muslim*, 2932a.

[124] *Musnad al-Imām Aḥmad*, 26425.

[125] *Musnad al-Imām Aḥmad*, 26426.

20
She is a Guardian

عَنْ عَبْدِ اللَّهِ بْنِ عُمَرَ رَضِيَ اللَّهُ عَنْهُمَا أَنَّ رَسُولَ اللهِ صَلَّى اللَّهُ عَلَيْهِ وَسَلَّمَ قَالَ:

أَلا كُلُّكُمْ رَاعٍ وَكُلُّكُمْ مَسْئُولٌ عَنْ رَعِيَّتِهِ فَالْإِمَامُ الَّذِي عَلَى النَّاسِ رَاعٍ وَهُوَ مَسْئُولٌ عَنْ رَعِيَّتِهِ وَالرَّجُلُ رَاعٍ عَلَى أَهْلِ بَيْتِهِ وَهُوَ مَسْئُولٌ عَنْ رَعِيَّتِهِ وَالْمَرْأَةُ رَاعِيَةٌ عَلَى أَهْلِ بَيْتِ زَوْجِهَا وَوَلَدِهِ وَهِيَ مَسْئُولَةٌ عَنْهُمْ وَعَبْدُ الرَّجُلِ رَاعٍ عَلَى مَالِ سَيِّدِهِ وَهُوَ مَسْئُولٌ عَنْهُ أَلَا فَكُلُّكُمْ رَاعٍ وَكُلُّكُمْ مَسْئُولٌ عَنْ رَعِيَّتِهِ.

ʿAbdullāh ibn ʿUmar narrated that Allah's Messenger ﷺ said:

"Every one of you is a shepherd and is responsible for his flock. The leader of the people is a guardian and is responsible for his subjects. A man is the guardian of his family and he is responsible for them. A woman is the guardian of her husband's home and children, and she is responsible for them. The servant of a man is a guardian of his property and is responsible for it. No doubt, every one of you is a shepherd and is responsible for his flock."[126]

Every one of us is a guardian of something, or someone. Whether we are the master or the servant, the leader or the follower, the employer or the employee, each of us are guardians and each of us are responsible, and therefore accountable, for what we guard. It is no different in the marital home. A man is responsible for his family as a whole; his wife is responsible for the home, their children, herself, and his wealth.

It is the responsibility of every woman to look after the household that she has been put in charge of. Islamic society encourages men to go out and earn a living to bring wealth back to the family and ensure their survival. This is a duty that men must fulfil *as men.* Likewise, Islamic society encourages women to remain within their house as much as possible and manage the home from there. The saying 'an Englishman's home is his castle' comes to mind here, though perhaps

[126] *Ṣaḥīḥ al-Bukhārī,* 7138; *Ṣaḥīḥ Muslim,* 1829.

it would be more suitable to say 'a Muslim woman's home is her fortress.'

She must ensure that the finances made available to her by her husband can be properly distributed to ensure the upkeep of the home, ensure food and warmth are provided, and the members of the household are well-looked after. She must care for their children. As we mentioned earlier, the nurturing of the children is both her right and her duty. She must look after them physically by protecting them from potential danger while they are in her lone charge, mentally by schooling them and teaching them about life and the wider world, and spiritually by teaching them the fundamentals of Islam, *īmān,* and *iḥsān.*[127]

As mentioned previously, Sayyidunā Abū Hurayrah ﵁ narrated:

قِيلَ لِرَسُولِ اللَّهِ صلى الله عليه وسلم أَيُّ النِّسَاءِ خَيْرٌ؟

قَالَ الَّتِي تَسُرُّهُ إِذَا نَظَرَ وَتُطِيعُهُ إِذَا أَمَرَ وَلاَ تُخَالِفُهُ فِي نَفْسِهَا وَمَالِهَا بِمَا يَكْرَهُ.

"It was asked of Allah's Messenger ﷺ, 'Which woman is best?'

He replied, 'The one who pleases him when he looks at her, obeys him when he commands her, and does not go against his wishes with regard to herself nor her wealth.'"[128]

It should suffice to say that a woman must ensure that, just as the house, the finances and wealth, and their children should be looked after, so too should she look after herself. A woman must protect herself from any situation that could call her honour into question.

---

[127] Islam is worshipping Allah alone, praying the daily *ṣalāh,* paying *zakāh,* fasting throughout Ramadan, and the Hajj. *Īmān* is belief in Allah, His Angels, His books, His Messengers, the Last Day, that fate – both good and bad – is from Allah, and the life after death. *Iḥsān* is the state of worshipping Allah as if you can see Him, and if this is not possible then at least to worship Him in the knowledge that He sees you. See the 'Hadith of Jibrīl' ﵇ for further information. There have been many commentaries written on this hadith alone, and rightly so, for it encompasses the entire religion.

[128] *Sunan al-Nasāʾī,* 3231.

This also includes bettering herself physically, mentally, and spiritually, ensuring that she falls into the category of the best of women:

الْوَدُودُ الْوَلُودُ الْمُوَاتِيَةُ الْمُوَاسِيَةُ إِذَا اتَّقَيْنَ اللَّهَ

"... loving, fertile, favourable, and comforting, and they fear Allah."[129]

Sayyidunā 'Abdullāh ibn 'Abbās ؓ narrates that Allah's Messenger ﷺ said,

لَا يَخْلُوَنَّ رَجُلٌ بِامْرَأَةٍ وَلَا تُسَافِرَنَّ امْرَأَةٌ إِلَّا وَمَعَهَا مَحْرَمٌ.
فَقَامَ رَجُلٌ فَقَالَ يَا رَسُولَ اللَّهِ اكْتُتِبْتُ فِي غَزْوَةِ كَذَا وَكَذَا وَخَرَجَتْ امْرَأَتِي حَاجَّةً.
قَالَ اذْهَبْ فَحُجَّ مَعَ امْرَأَتِكَ.

"A man should not be alone with a woman, nor should a woman travel except with a guardian."

A man stood up and said, "O Allah's Messenger, I have been assigned to such and such a military expedition, but my wife has already left for the Hajj."

The Prophet ﷺ said, "Go and perform the Hajj with your wife."[130]

The guardianship of a woman's honour is not reserved for the home alone, but also applies to the road and wherever it leads. A woman is not to travel without a guardian with her, meaning her husband or an un-marriable male member of her family. A person is considered a traveller when they have left the limits of their town or city and have travelled a distance of 80 kilometres (or 50 miles). In general, we should always err on the side of caution and thus even shorter distances should be negotiated with a chaperone.

In our current day and age, it has become all too common for women to commute to their place of education or work alone, or to go on 'girl's holidays' overseas with their female friends. Such behaviour

---

[129] *Al-Sunan al-Kubrā*, 12480.
[130] *Ṣaḥīḥ al-Bukhārī*, 3006; *Ṣaḥīḥ Muslim*, 1341.

invites the potential of needless suspicion and increases the likelihood of dangerous situations. Even so-called Islamic households are not spared from these issues, with young men and women spending time alone together when in college away from the view of their parents, and sisters travelling long distances to sit in mixed gatherings for the purpose of 'Islamic education and reminders'.

What benefit is an Islamic reminder when you have to forget your Islamic principles to be reminded in the first place?

3 | THE SELF-AWARE WOMAN

21
She is Feminine

عَنِ ابْنِ عَبَّاسٍ - رضى الله عنهما - قَالَ:

لَعَنَ رَسُولُ اللَّهِ صلى الله عليه وسلم الْمُتَشَبِّهِينَ مِنَ الرِّجَالِ بِالنِّسَاءِ، وَالْمُتَشَبِّهَاتِ مِنَ النِّسَاءِ بِالرِّجَالِ.

Ibn ʿAbbās ﷺ said:

"Allah's Messenger ﷺ cursed those men who behaved like women and those women who behaved like men."[181]

We have arrived at what is sadly the most topical subject of our age. Up until very recently the idea that a good woman was feminine went without saying. Yet here we are, discussing femininity itself as a quality that a woman should exhibit.

Femininity is the opposite of masculinity. For decades, western secular liberalism has been pushing society towards a *transhumanist singularity*, when society's march of progressivism will swell until it passes beyond a point of no return, and the change that secular liberalism seeks to wreak upon the world becomes irreversible and near-infinitely transgressive. What began as a questioning of gender roles soon progressed to questioning normative sexual practices, then

---

[181] *Ṣaḥīḥ al-Bukhārī*, 5885.

sexuality as a whole. This trend has continued throughout the last century until we have reached a point where 'heteronormativity' itself is being questioned,[132] where sexuality is a spectrum, and where people question the truth of binary genders. As time goes on, we move further away from normative human practices and closer and closer to transhumanism.

The question of what it means to be human has moved away from the realm of philosophy and morality and has become a question of physicality. In a godless worldview, where the soul does not exist, where there is no objective truth, where morality is subject to the whims and desires of the people in any given time (and can then be applied retrospectively to make heroes into villains and villains into heroes), and where desires are divine and True Divinity is labelled false, there is nothing to anchor oneself to. A human is anything you want it to be. Can only women give birth? Can we choose exactly who a child will be *prior* to conception? Do we need flesh and bone to be called human at all, or can we encase ourselves in steel forms limited only by our imaginations, or upload our consciousness into quettabytes of information, and still be called human if we so desire? Once these questions were the stuff of science fiction; now they are genuinely being asked.

All of this is the result of the proliferation of non-normative behaviour which the Prophet ﷺ warned us against centuries ago. Islam ensures that the basic communal ideas and norms that *fiṭrah* dictates (such as the family, heterosexuality, gender roles and the binary of masculinity and femininity, and belief in the Oneness of Allah) are unchanging and constant. Society *needs* constants to anchor itself with; without them there is no truth. The truth of the fundamentals of existence, of physics, logic, and mathematics, requires order and constancy.

---

[132] It is this very questioning of the idea that led to the coining of the term in 'queer theory', as prior to this it did not require a term. It just was.

A woman is feminine. This book as a whole defines what it means to be a feminine woman, and the section covering a woman's relationship with herself has begun with the hadith above to remind you, dear sister, that your beauty and your value does not lie in your physical appearance, your level of education, your job title, or whatever 'number' that unmanly men may describe you with. It is found in your adherence to the core principles, characteristics, manners, and ideas that are intrinsic to your existence as a woman, and in your adherence to Islam. There is greatness to be found in womanhood and, though many have forgotten what greatness is, Islam continues to remind us how great each of us can be.

Sayyidah Ḥawwā', Sayyidah Maryam, Sayyidah Āsiyah, the Ummahāt al-Mu'minīn, the Ṣaḥābiyāt: were these women not deserving of the title of greatness?

If greatness is what you seek, then turn to Islam for it. If truth is what you seek, turn to Allah. Each of us seeks goodness and success. Neither can be achieved without following the Commands of Allah and the way of His Messenger.

Sayyidunā Anas narrates that Allah's Messenger said,

حُبِّبَ إِلَيَّ مِنَ الدُّنْيَا النِّسَاءُ وَالطِّيبُ وَجُعِلَ قُرَّةُ عَيْنِي فِي الصَّلَاةِ.

"In this world, women and perfume have been made dear to me, and my comfort has been provided in prayer."[133]

There is nothing more endearing or beautiful in a woman than her femininity itself: her compassion, her mercy, her kindness, her softness, her inner courage and strength, her nurturing, calming, and comforting nature, her honourable behaviour, her modesty, and her grace... Femininity is a dear and precious thing. Hold onto it with both hands, for there are those who seek to take it from you.

[133] *Sunan al-Nasā'ī*, 3939.

22
She is Altruistic

عن عائشة قَالَتْ:

جَاءَتْنِي امْرَأَةٌ وَمَعَهَا ابْنَتَانِ لَهَا فَسَأَلَتْنِي فَلَمْ تَجِدْ عِنْدِي شَيْئًا غَيْرَ تَمْرَةٍ وَاحِدَةٍ فَأَعْطَيْتُهَا إِيَّاهَا فَأَخَذَتْهَا فَقَسَمَتْهَا بَيْنَ ابْنَتَيْهَا وَلَمْ تَأْكُلْ مِنْهَا شَيْئًا ثُمَّ قَامَتْ فَخَرَجَتْ وَابْنَتَاهَا فَدَخَلَ عَلَيَّ النَّبِيُّ صَلَّى اللَّهُ عَلَيْهِ وَسَلَّمَ فَحَدَّثْتُهُ حَدِيثَهَا فَقَالَ النَّبِيُّ صَلَّى اللَّهُ عَلَيْهِ وَسَلَّمَ مَنْ ابْتُلِيَ مِنْ الْبَنَاتِ بِشَيْءٍ فَأَحْسَنَ إِلَيْهِنَّ كُنَّ لَهُ سِتْرًا مِنْ النَّارِ

'Ā'ishah ؓ narrates:

"A woman came to me asking for charity and with her were her two daughters. She found nothing with me except a single date. I gave it to her and she divided it between her two daughters, and ate nothing of it herself. She then stood and left. The Prophet ﷺ entered and I told him her story. The Prophet ﷺ said, 'Whoever is tested with daughters in any way and treats them well, they will be his shield against the Hellfire.'"[184]

Altruism is the disregarding of one's own interests for the sake of another. It is the core quality of the selfless, those who put others before themselves, who choose self-sacrifice over causing others difficulty. A Muslimah must develop this quality within herself if she wishes to become a great woman, for the great women of Islam all possessed this quality. And why would they not? If women are empathetic supporters, nurturers, and carers, would not the best of them be altruistic by definition? Altruism is the greatest form of supporting others, for it involves putting one's interest aside for the interest of another, without any hope of reward or a return on investment. The giving is purely to please Allah, and thus Allah will please them in the Hereafter:

---

[184] *Saḥīḥ al-Bukhārī*, 5649; *Saḥīḥ Muslim*, 2629.

$$\text{وَسَيُجَنَّبُهَا ٱلْأَتْقَى (١٧) ٱلَّذِى يُؤْتِى مَالَهُۥ يَتَزَكَّىٰ (١٨) وَمَا لِأَحَدٍ عِندَهُۥ مِن نِّعْمَةٍ تُجْزَىٰٓ (١٩) إِلَّا ٱبْتِغَآءَ وَجْهِ رَبِّهِ ٱلْأَعْلَىٰ (٢٠) وَلَسَوْفَ يَرْضَىٰ (٢١)}$$

> "But the righteous will be spared from it (the Raging Fire) – those who donate of their wealth only to purify themselves, not in return for someone's favours, but seeking the pleasure of their Lord, the Most High. They will certainly be pleased."[135]

Umm al-Mu'minīn Sayyidah ʿĀ'ishah[136] had but one date in her home when her sister came to her door, because the Prophet and his household would not hoard wealth or stockpile food. If there was no immediate need for it, they would spend it on others. Altruism was their way. So, when Umm al-Mu'minīn Sayyidah ʿĀ'ishah was asked for help, it was not in her nature to refuse someone in need, despite only having a single date to eat herself. She gave the date to the woman, who sacrificed her own hunger to feed her children what little she had. Umm al-Mu'minīn Sayyidah ʿĀ'ishah also said:

$$\text{إِنْ كُنَّا آلَ مُحَمَّدٍ صلى الله عليه وسلم لَنَمْكُثُ شَهْرًا مَا نَسْتَوْقِدُ بِنَارٍ إِنْ هُوَ إِلَّا التَّمْرُ وَالْمَاءُ.}$$

> "We, the wives of Muhammad, used to spend a whole month without kindling the fire.[137] We had naught but dates and water."[138]

These are the women who were chosen to live alongside Allah's Messenger, and were blessed to be among those about whom Allah says:

$$\text{جَزَآؤُهُمْ عِندَ رَبِّهِمْ جَنَّٰتُ عَدْنٍ تَجْرِى مِن تَحْتِهَا ٱلْأَنْهَٰرُ خَٰلِدِينَ فِيهَآ أَبَدًا ۖ رَّضِىَ ٱللَّهُ عَنْهُمْ وَرَضُوا۟ عَنْهُ ۚ ذَٰلِكَ لِمَنْ خَشِىَ رَبَّهُۥ (٨)}$$

---

[135] Qur'an, 92:17-21.
[136] Interestingly, the verses from Sūrah al-Layl above were revealed in relation to her father. It is no surprise, when her blessed husband was the greatest of the Prophets and her noble father was the greatest man after the Prophets, that she came to be among the greatest of women.
[137] Meaning that they had no need to, as there was nothing to cook.
[138] Ṣaḥīḥ Muslim, 2972a.

"Their reward with their Lord will be Gardens of Eternity, under which rivers flow, to stay there forever and ever. Allah is pleased with them and they are pleased with Him. This is for those in awe of their Lord."[139]

To be altruistic is itself a blessing from Allah, for the one who is blessed with this quality fears neither poverty nor death, cares little for the world, and earns her Hereafter through self-sacrifice and giving. Allah says:

إِنَّ ٱلْمُصَّدِّقِينَ وَٱلْمُصَّدِّقَٰتِ وَأَقْرَضُوا۟ ٱللَّهَ قَرْضًا حَسَنًا يُضَٰعَفُ لَهُمْ وَلَهُمْ أَجْرٌ كَرِيمٌ (١٨)

"Indeed, those men and women who give in charity and lend to Allah a good loan will have it multiplied for them, and they will have an honourable reward."[140]

The Ṣaḥābiyāt ﵅ understood that the world was transient and the Hereafter would be a residence of permanence. When you have complete belief in this fact, why would you not give up what is ephemeral for what is forever? Sayyidunā Abū Hurayrah ﵁ narrated:

جَاءَ رَجُلٌ إِلَى رَسُولِ اللَّهِ صلى الله عليه وسلم فَقَالَ: إِنِّي مَجْهُودٌ. فَأَرْسَلَ إِلَى بَعْضِ نِسَائِهِ، فَقَالَتْ: وَالَّذِي بَعَثَكَ بِالْحَقِّ، مَا عِنْدِي إِلاَّ مَاءٌ . ثُمَّ أَرْسَلَ إِلَى أُخْرَى، فَقَالَتْ: مِثْلَ ذَلِكَ حَتَّى قُلْنَ كُلُّهُنَّ مِثْلَ ذَلِكَ لاَ وَالَّذِي بَعَثَكَ بِالْحَقِّ مَا عِنْدِي إِلاَّ مَاءٌ .

فَقَالَ: مَنْ يُضِيفُ هَذَا اللَّيْلَةَ رَحِمَهُ اللَّهُ. فَقَامَ رَجُلٌ مِنَ الأَنْصَارِ فَقَالَ: أَنَا يَا رَسُولَ اللَّهِ . فَانْطَلَقَ بِهِ إِلَى رَحْلِهِ فَقَالَ لاِمْرَأَتِهِ هَلْ عِنْدَكِ شَىْءٌ . قَالَتْ لاَ إِلاَّ قُوتُ صِبْيَانِي . قَالَ: فَعَلِّلِيهِمْ بِشَىْءٍ فَإِذَا دَخَلَ ضَيْفُنَا فَأَطْفِئِي السِّرَاجَ وَأَرِيهِ أَنَّا نَأْكُلُ فَإِذَا أَهْوَى لِيَأْكُلَ فَقُومِي إِلَى السِّرَاجِ حَتَّى تُطْفِئِيهِ . قَالَ: فَقَعَدُوا وَأَكَلَ الضَّيْفُ . فَلَمَّا أَصْبَحَ غَدَا عَلَى النَّبِيِّ صلى الله عليه وسلم فَقَالَ: قَدْ عَجِبَ اللَّهُ مِنْ صَنِيعِكُمَا بِضَيْفِكُمَا اللَّيْلَةَ.

"A person came to Allah's Messenger ﷺ and said, 'I am starving.' He sent for one of his wives, but she said, 'By He Who sent you with Truth, I have naught with me but water.' He then sent for another wife, and she gave the same reply, until all of them gave the same

[139] Qur'an, 98:8.
[140] Qur'an, 57:18.

reply, *'By He Who sent you with Truth, I have naught with me but water.'*

The Prophet ﷺ said, *'Whoever entertains this guest tonight, Allah will shower him with mercy.'* A man from the Anṣār[141] stood and said, *'I will, O Allah's Messenger.'* He took him to his house and asked his wife, *'Do you have anything?'* She replied, *'No, only a little for our children.'* He said, *'Distract them with something. When the guest enters, extinguish the lamp, and pretend that we are eating.'* So they sat and the guest had his meal. The next morning, he went to Allah's Messenger ﷺ, who said, *'Allah was well-pleased with what you both did for your guest last night.'*"[142]

From this we can see that the situation of Umm al-Mu'minīn Sayyidah ʿĀ'ishah ؓ with regard to not having food in the house was not particular to her, but a common situation in the household of the Prophet ﷺ. The Ṣaḥābah ؓ had such genuine love for their fellow Muslims that they were willing to sacrifice the last of their food, even allowing their children to go hungry that night, just so their struggling guest could eat. It was about this incident that Allah revealed the following verse:

وَٱلَّذِينَ تَبَوَّءُو ٱلدَّارَ وَٱلْإِيمَٰنَ مِن قَبْلِهِمْ يُحِبُّونَ مَنْ هَاجَرَ إِلَيْهِمْ وَلَا يَجِدُونَ فِى صُدُورِهِمْ حَاجَةً مِّمَّآ أُوتُواْ وَيُؤْثِرُونَ عَلَىٰٓ أَنفُسِهِمْ وَلَوْ كَانَ بِهِمْ خَصَاصَةٌ ۚ وَمَن يُوقَ شُحَّ نَفْسِهِۦ فَأُوْلَٰٓئِكَ هُمُ ٱلْمُفْلِحُونَ (٩)

"As for those who had settled in the city and (embraced) the faith before the emigrants, they love whoever immigrates to them, never having a desire in their hearts for whatever is given to the emigrants. They give preference over themselves even though they may be in need. And whoever is saved from the selfishness of their own souls, it is they who are successful."[143]

---

[141] Sayyidunā Abū Ṭalḥah al-Anṣārī ؓ.
[142] *Ṣaḥīḥ Muslim*, 2054.
[143] Qur'an, 59:9.

23
She is Modest

عَنْ أُمِّ سَلَمَةَ قَالَتْ:

بَيْنَا نَحْنُ عِنْدَ رَسُولِ اللَّهِ صَلَّى اللَّهُ عَلَيْهِ وَسَلَّمَ أَقْبَلَ ابْنُ أُمِّ مَكْتُومٍ فَدَخَلَ عَلَيْهِ وَذَلِكَ بَعْدَ مَا أُمِرْنَا بِالْحِجَابِ فَقَالَ رَسُولُ اللَّهِ صَلَّى اللَّهُ عَلَيْهِ وَسَلَّمَ احْتَجِبَا مِنْهُ فَقُلْتُ يَا رَسُولَ اللَّهِ أَلَيْسَ هُوَ أَعْمَى لَا يُبْصِرُنَا وَلَا يَعْرِفُنَا فَقَالَ رَسُولُ اللَّهِ صَلَّى اللَّهُ عَلَيْهِ وَسَلَّمَ أَفَعَمْيَاوَانِ أَنْتُمَا أَلَسْتُمَا تُبْصِرَانِهِ

Umm Salamah narrated:

"While we were with Allah's Messenger ﷺ, Ibn Umm Maktūm[144] was given permission to enter, and this was after the command to veil. The Prophet ﷺ said, 'Veil yourselves from him.' I said, 'O Allah's Messenger, is he not blind? He cannot see or recognise us.' The Prophet ﷺ said, 'Are you blind? Can you not see him?'"[145]

Modesty has almost become a thing of the past. The Muslim women of today hold eye contact with men, are forward in their conversations, and care little for the legal rulings against intermingling and *khalwah.*[146] Yet Muslim women, as weak as they have become in this regard, are still known across the world for their modesty, for the condition of women as a whole has become so weak that even when the manners of the Muslimah have fallen they still far outshine those of others.

Modesty is the cloak that a Muslimah enshrouds herself in, protecting her from the gazes and judgement of strange men. She draws the hood of humility over her head and veils herself with shyness. Her manners are a shield that guard her from evil eyes and false tongues, and though she may stand to the side amongst the

---

[144] Sayyidunā ʿAbdullāh ibn Umm Maktūm ﷺ.
[145] *Jāmiʿ al-Tirmidhī*, 2278.
[146] Being alone with a non-*mahram* member of the opposite sex.

shadows for fear of drawing unwanted attention to herself, in the Sight of Allah she is a shining beacon of faith. Allah says:

وَقُل لِّلْمُؤْمِنَـٰتِ يَغْضُضْنَ مِنْ أَبْصَـٰرِهِنَّ وَيَحْفَظْنَ فُرُوجَهُنَّ وَلَا يُبْدِينَ زِينَتَهُنَّ إِلَّا مَا
ظَهَرَ مِنْهَا ۖ وَلْيَضْرِبْنَ بِخُمُرِهِنَّ عَلَىٰ جُيُوبِهِنَّ ۖ وَلَا يُبْدِينَ زِينَتَهُنَّ إِلَّا لِبُعُولَتِهِنَّ أَوْ ءَابَآئِهِنَّ أَوْ
ءَابَآءِ بُعُولَتِهِنَّ أَوْ أَبْنَآئِهِنَّ أَوْ أَبْنَآءِ بُعُولَتِهِنَّ أَوْ إِخْوَٰنِهِنَّ أَوْ بَنِىٓ إِخْوَٰنِهِنَّ أَوْ بَنِىٓ أَخَوَٰتِهِنَّ أَوْ
نِسَآئِهِنَّ أَوْ مَا مَلَكَتْ أَيْمَـٰنُهُنَّ أَوِ ٱلتَّـٰبِعِينَ غَيْرِ أُو۟لِى ٱلْإِرْبَةِ مِنَ ٱلرِّجَالِ أَوِ ٱلطِّفْلِ ٱلَّذِينَ لَمْ
يَظْهَرُوا۟ عَلَىٰ عَوْرَٰتِ ٱلنِّسَآءِ ۖ وَلَا يَضْرِبْنَ بِأَرْجُلِهِنَّ لِيُعْلَمَ مَا يُخْفِينَ مِن زِينَتِهِنَّ ۚ وَتُوبُوٓا۟ إِلَى
ٱللَّهِ جَمِيعًا أَيُّهَ ٱلْمُؤْمِنُونَ لَعَلَّكُمْ تُفْلِحُونَ (٣١)

"And tell the believing women to lower their gaze and guard their chastity, and not to reveal their adornments except what normally appears. Let them draw their veils over their chests, and not reveal their adornments except to their husbands, their fathers, their fathers-in-law, their sons, their stepsons, their brothers, their brothers' sons or sisters' sons, their fellow women, those in their possession, male attendants with no desire, or children who are still unaware of women's nakedness. Let them not stomp their feet, drawing attention to their hidden adornments. Turn to Allah in repentance all together, O believers, so that you may be successful."[147]

The Muslimah does not raise her voice needlessly and does not soften it when forced by circumstances to speak to men. She does not unveil her beauty to anyone except the one she has accepted to be her partner in this life and the next, and she does not perfume and beautify herself for anyone else but him. When women leave the house wearing jewellery and make-up they say, "I am doing this for *me*," as if the mirror is the only reason they are dressed up, as if they would think less of themselves if they did not please their own eyes. Make-up, tight-fitting and immodest clothing, and jewellery are only meant for one purpose: for others to see you and be impressed. High heels are designed to make you appear taller, your feet appear smaller, your legs appear longer, and to announce your arrival from a distance; their *click-click-click* says only one thing: "Look this way, I am coming."

---

[147] Qur'an, 24:31.

Tight clothes are designed to accentuate your figure and display it to the world. Make-up is but a ruse to artificially beautify oneself and attract others toward you, making one's appearance more enticing and implying fertility. Jewellery beautifies the one wearing it, its glamour and shine placed strategically on the body to draw the eye. If worn for one's spouse behind closed doors, all of these beautifiers are praiseworthy things; if worn outside, they are accursed. A Muslimah strives for humility, whereas wearing such things in public highlights her pride.

It is also common practice now for women to wear strong perfumes when they leave the house. For whom is this benefit? The defensive ones will no doubt repeat the mantra "I do it for *me*," but again this is quite clearly untrue. Perfume is for the benefit of others. Women's perfumes are designed to attract the eyes of men towards the wearer. If the smell alone is beautiful, then how beautiful must the wearer be? Sayyidunā Abū Mūsā ؓ narrates that the Prophet ﷺ said,

كُلُّ عَيْنٍ زَانِيَةٌ وَالْمَرْأَةُ إِذَا اسْتَعْطَرَتْ فَمَرَّتْ بِالْمَجْلِسِ فَهِيَ كَذَا وَكَذَا يَعْنِي زَانِيَةٌ

"Every eye can commit adultery. The woman who adorns herself with perfumes to pass by an assembly of men is as such and such," meaning an adulteress.[148]

A woman that seeks to entice men with her scent, her garb, her beauty, or her actions is as much an adulteress as the one who takes these matters to their ultimate conclusion. Sayyidunā Abū Hurayrah ؓ said:

نِسَاءٌ كَاسِيَاتٌ عَارِيَاتٌ مَائِلَاتٌ مُمِيلَاتٌ لَا يَدْخُلْنَ الْجَنَّةَ وَلَا يَجِدْنَ رِيحَهَا وَرِيحُهَا يُوجَدُ مِنْ مَسِيرَةِ خَمْسِ مِائَةِ عَامٍ

"Some women are clothed but naked, they incline to evil and are seductresses. They will not enter Paradise nor even smell its

---

[148] *Jāmi' al-Tirmidhī*, 2786.

fragrance, though its fragrance can be found from five hundred years of travel away."[149]

Clothed, but naked. The fashion of today leaves nothing to the imagination. A woman can show no skin at all, and yet show her entire body. Non-Muslim women wear yoga pants, leggings, and tight fitting shirts, and our Muslimah sisters see them and denounce what they do. But have they looked at what they are wearing themselves? Have they held their own mode of dress up against the Islamic standards? If the shape of your legs or arms can be seen or guessed, you are not adhering to the Islamic model; if your hips, waist, shoulders, or chest are accentuated you are not modestly dressed. Hijab is not merely a cloth that covers your hair.

Men that see any part of you will imagine the rest; this is the weakness of men. Some men will try to argue to the contrary, but as Shakespeare would say they "*protest too much.*"

A Muslimah's shyness should be much more than this. Sayyidunā Abū al-Malīḥ al-Hudhalī ﵁ narrated:

أَنَّ نِسَاءً مِنْ أَهْلِ حِمْصَ أَوْ مِنْ أَهْلِ الشَّامِ دَخَلْنَ عَلَى عَائِشَةَ فَقَالَتْ أَنْتُنَّ اللاَّتِي يَدْخُلْنَ نِسَاؤُكُمُ الْحَمَّامَاتِ سَمِعْتُ رَسُولَ اللهِ صَلَّى اللهُ عَلَيْهِ وَسَلَّمَ يَقُولُ مَا مِنِ امْرَأَةٍ تَضَعُ أَثْيَابَهَا فِي غَيْرِ بَيْتِ زَوْجِهَا إِلَّا هَتَكَتِ السِّتْرَ بَيْنَهَا وَبَيْنَ رَبِّهَا

"Women from Homs or Syria entered the dwelling of ʿĀ'ishah, and she said, 'Are you those women who enter the bathhouses? I heard Allah's Messenger ﷺ say, "No woman lowers her clothes in a place other than her husband's home but that the barrier between her sin and her Lord will be torn to shreds."'"[150]

In another narration, Umm al-Mu'minīn Sayyidah Umm Salamah ﵂ narrated that Allah's Messenger ﷺ said:

أَيُّمَا امْرَأَةٍ نَزَعَتْ ثِيَابَهَا فِي غَيْرِ بَيْتِهَا خَرَقَ اللهُ عَنْهَا سِتْرًا

[149] Mālik ibn Anas, *Muwaṭṭa' Imām Mālik*, 1694.
[150] *Jāmiʿ al-Tirmidhī*, 2803.

"Whenever a woman removes her clothes outside of her home, Allah will tear open the barrier hiding her sin."[151]

A Muslimah's shyness does not allow her to fall into this behaviour. Even amongst womenfolk, she does not show her body. In the cultures we live in today, this should go without saying, as the level of depravity that is now considered normal ensures that women are acutely aware that it is not only the *male* gaze that seeks to unclothe them. Despite this, we still find sisters visiting hammams in the Middle East, removing all but a towel as they bathe and are bathed amongst other women.

In contrast, Umm al-Mu'minīn Sayyidah ʿĀ'ishah ﵂ said of the Ṣaḥābiyāt ﵅:

يَرْحَمُ اللَّهُ نِسَاءَ الْمُهَاجِرَاتِ الْأُوَلَ لَمَّا أَنْزَلَ اللَّهُ: 'وَلْيَضْرِبْنَ بِخُمُرِهِنَّ عَلَى جُيُوبِهِنَّ' شَقَّقْنَ مُرُوطَهُنَّ فَاخْتَمَرْنَ بِهَا.

"May Allah have mercy on the foremost women of the Muhājirūn. When Allah revealed the verse, 'Let them draw their veils over their chests,'[152] *they cut their sheets and veiled themselves with them."*[153]

A Muslimah's nobility lies not in a crown nor the finery of her clothes but in her modesty. The nobility of the Ṣaḥābiyāt ﵅ was unparalleled; seek your own by following them.

---

[151] *Musnad al-Imām Aḥmad*, 26569.
[152] Qur'an, 24:31.
[153] *Ṣaḥīḥ al-Bukhārī*, 4758.

24
She is Fit and Well

عَنْ عَائِشَةَ قَالَتْ كَانَ رَسُولُ اللهِ صَلَّى اللهُ عَلَيْهِ وَسَلَّمَ يَقُولُ:

اللَّهُمَّ عَافِنِي فِي جَسَدِي وَعَافِنِي فِي بَصَرِي وَاجْعَلْهُ الْوَارِثَ مِنِّي لَا إِلَهَ إِلَّا اللهُ الْحَلِيمُ الْكَرِيمُ سُبْحَانَ اللهِ رَبِّ الْعَرْشِ الْعَظِيمِ وَالْحَمْدُ لِلَّهِ رَبِّ الْعَالَمِينَ

ʿĀ'ishah reported that Allah's Messenger ﷺ used to say:

"O Allah, grant me wellness in my body, wellness in my sight, and make my sight endure within me. There is none worthy of worship except Allah, the Forbearing, the Generous. Glory be to Allah, the Lord of the Great Throne. All praise is due to Allah, the Lord of the Worlds."[154]

A Muslim asks Allah for wellness and health in this life and the next, for nothing can be achieved except by His decree alone. The Prophet ﷺ would pray for the wellness of his body, despite it being the picture of health, and that of his eyesight, despite his vision being greater than, and far beyond the scope of, any other human being. For example, there is a narration of Sayyidunā Anas ؓ where prior to the first *takbīr* of *ṣalāh* the Prophet ﷺ said, "*Straighten your rows and close your ranks, for I can see you from behind my back.*"[155] The gifts he had received from Allah did not preclude him from asking for more grace and aid from Allah. We should bear this in mind: the bounties of Allah are infinite, and His coffers are never emptied. Ask from Him and you shall receive, pray to Him and He shall be pleased with you.

However, as Muslims, we do not simply pray to Allah and await the outcome. We ask for His Divine Aid and Guidance and then we *work* towards achieving our goals. This has always been the path to acceptance. As Muslims, we should strengthen our bodies, build our stamina and agility, and hone our bodies as well as we hone our minds.

---

[154] *Jāmiʿ al-Tirmidhī*, 3480.
[155] *Ṣaḥīḥ al-Bukhārī*, 719, 725; *Sunan al-Nasāʾī*, 814, 845.

Just because someone is female, this does not mean that she should allow herself to be weak and frail. The Ṣaḥābiyāt ﷺ were not frail women. They lived hard lives and ensured that they did not become weak from excessive worship - not by lessening their worship, but by remaining physically active. As we have previously quoted, Sayyidunā ʿAlī ﷺ described his wife, Sayyidah Fāṭimah ﷺ, thus:

إِنَّهَا جَرَّتْ بِالرَّحَى حَتَّى أَثَّرَ فِي يَدِهَا وَاسْتَقَتْ بِالْقِرْبَةِ حَتَّى أَثَّرَ فِي نَحْرِهَا وَكَنَسَتِ الْبَيْتَ حَتَّى اغْبَرَّتْ ثِيَابُهَا

"She turned the millstone until it calloused her hand, she carried the waterskin until it marked the upper portion of her chest, and she swept the house until her clothes became dirty."[156]

These are not the actions of a weak woman. If she was not fit and well, she would not be able to do these tasks. In fact, tasks such as these make the doer fitter and stronger. Sayyidunā Abū Hurayrah ﷺ narrates that Allah's Messenger ﷺ said,

الْمُؤْمِنُ الْقَوِيُّ خَيْرٌ وَأَحَبُّ إِلَى اللهِ مِنَ الْمُؤْمِنِ الضَّعِيفِ وَفِي كُلٍّ خَيْرٌ احْرِصْ عَلَى مَا يَنْفَعُكَ وَاسْتَعِنْ بِاللهِ وَلاَ تَعْجِزْ وَإِنْ أَصَابَكَ شَيْءٌ فَلاَ تَقُلْ لَوْ أَنِّي فَعَلْتُ كَانَ كَذَا وَكَذَا. وَلَكِنْ قُلْ قَدَرُ اللهِ وَمَا شَاءَ فَعَلَ فَإِنَّ لَوْ تَفْتَحُ عَمَلَ الشَّيْطَانِ.

"A strong believer is better and more lovable to Allah than a weak believer, and there is good in everyone. Cherish that which gives you benefit in the Hereafter, seek help from Allah, and do not lose heart. If anything occurs, do not say, 'If I had done that then such and such would not have occurred.' Rather, say, 'Allah did this, and He did as He ordained.' Your 'ifs' open the door for Shayṭān."[157]

Part of self-care is to beautify oneself, and a woman can and should do this for her husband. But beautification is not restricted to the artificial kind. A woman should also seek beauty in her own physical form. Our bodies are not our own but loaned to us by Allah[158] and each

---

[156] *Sunan Abī Dāwūd*, 2988.

[157] *Ṣaḥīḥ Muslim*, 2664.

[158] This is a key difference between Islamic and secular thinking, as the secular liberals believe in the inherent goodness of self-pleasure and individualism, whereas Muslims

of us thus has a responsibility to care for our bodies and ensure that they are the best form they can be. Being overweight due to gluttony is not praiseworthy in Islam, though the modern Western world seeks to make such thinking common amongst the masses. There is therefore no harm in a woman seeking to hone her body through exercise, though care should be taken to ensure the rules of hijab are not broken. Yet, along with this beautification and care for our bodies comes a further responsibility. Umm al-Mu'minīn Sayyidah ʿĀ'ishah ﵂ narrates:

أَنَّ أَسْمَاءَ بِنْتَ أَبِي بَكْرٍ دَخَلَتْ عَلَى رَسُولِ اللَّهِ صَلَّى اللَّهُ عَلَيْهِ وَسَلَّمَ وَعَلَيْهَا ثِيَابٌ رِقَاقٌ فَأَعْرَضَ عَنْهَا رَسُولُ اللَّهِ صَلَّى اللَّهُ عَلَيْهِ وَسَلَّمَ وَقَالَ يَا أَسْمَاءُ إِنَّ الْمَرْأَةَ إِذَا بَلَغَتِ الْمَحِيضَ لَمْ تَصْلُحْ أَنْ يُرَى مِنْهَا إِلَّا هَذَا وَهَذَا وَأَشَارَ إِلَى وَجْهِهِ وَكَفَّيْهِ

"Asmā' bint Abū Bakr entered the house of Allah's Messenger ﷺ wearing a thin garment. Allah's Messenger ﷺ turned away from her and said, 'Asmā', when a woman reaches the age of maturity, it is not proper for her to show anything but this and this,' and the Prophet ﷺ pointed to his face and hands."[159]

Being from the household of a person does not allow one to loosen the restrictions and etiquettes with regard to one's beauty, nor does the piety or age of a person. A woman's beauty, like a jewel, has many facets to it. Her beauty is natural, physical, and spiritual, internal and external, both plain to see (in her actions) and coveted. Grace too is part of one's beauty and, like the body, can be honed and perfected. Sayyidah ʿĀ'ishah bint Ṭalḥah ﵂ narrates that Umm al-Mu'minīn Sayyidah ʿĀ'ishah ﵂ said,

مَا رَأَيْتُ أَحَدًا كَانَ أَشْبَهَ سَمْتًا وَهَدْيًا وَدَلاًّ بِرَسُولِ اللَّهِ صلى الله عليه وسلم مِنْ فَاطِمَةَ كَرَّمَ اللَّهُ وَجْهَهَا كَانَتْ إِذَا دَخَلَتْ عَلَيْهِ قَامَ إِلَيْهَا فَأَخَذَ بِيَدِهَا وَقَبَّلَهَا وَأَجْلَسَهَا فِي مَجْلِسِهِ وَكَانَ إِذَا دَخَلَ عَلَيْهَا قَامَتْ إِلَيْهِ فَأَخَذَتْ بِيَدِهِ فَقَبَّلَتْهُ وَأَجْلَسَتْهُ فِي مَجْلِسِهَا.

---

understand that even our bodies themselves do not belong to us, and all praise is for Allah alone. It is His pleasure we seek, not our own.

159 *Sunan Abī Dāwūd*, 4104.

"I saw no one more like Allah's Messenger ﷺ in respect of gravity, calmness, and pleasant disposition than Fāṭimah, may Allah ennoble her countenance. When she came to visit him, he would stand to welcome her, take her by the hand, kiss her, and sit her where he was sitting; and when he went to visit her, she would stand to welcome him, take him by the hand, kiss him, and sit him where she was sitting."[160]

Gracefulness is both an elegance in one's movement and a courteousness and honourability in one's behaviour. The Prophet ﷺ was the epitome of both, yet here we find that both his mannerisms and his manners were emulated most clearly by his beloved daughter, Sayyidah Fāṭimah ؓ. True beauty is found in one's character and comportment, in the grace of one's actions and deeds. A Muslimah must hone these too, for one can be the most beautiful woman in the world in features and physicality, and yet still be ugly in her actions and behaviour.

---

[160] *Sunan Abī Dāwūd*, 5217.

25
She Values Cleanliness and Self-Care

عَنْ جَابِرِ بْنِ عَبْدِ اللَّهِ ـ رضى الله عنهما ـ أَنَّ النَّبِيَّ صلى الله عليه وسلم قَالَ:

إِذَا دَخَلْتَ لَيْلاً فَلاَ تَدْخُلْ عَلَى أَهْلِكَ حَتَّى تَسْتَحِدَّ الْمُغِيبَةُ وَتَمْتَشِطَ الشَّعِثَةُ.

قَالَ قَالَ رَسُولُ اللَّهِ صلى الله عليه وسلم فَعَلَيْكَ بِالْكَيْسِ الْكَيْسِ.

Jābir ibn ʿAbdullāh ﵁ narrates that the Prophet ﷺ said:

"If you return from a journey at night, do not enter upon your family, to the extent that the woman whose husband was absent can shave and the dishevelled woman can comb."

Allah's Messenger ﷺ further stated, "Seek to have offspring, seek to have offspring!"[161]

Cleanliness and self-care (in the physical sense) are qualities that women still maintain today. A woman should seek to keep her body free of dirt and filth, and should be well-groomed, just as a man should be. Sayyidunā Saʿīd ibn al-Musayyib ﵀ said, "*Indeed Allah is good and He loves what is good, He is Clean and He loves cleanliness, He is Kind and He loves kindness, He is Generous and He loves generosity.*"[162] Cleanliness is thus paramount. Allah's Messenger ﷺ said,

الطُّهُورُ شَطْرُ الإِيمَانِ

"Cleanliness is part of faith."[163]

Allah Himself says:

وَٱللَّهُ يُحِبُّ ٱلْمُطَّهِّرِينَ

---

[161] *Ṣaḥīḥ al-Bukhārī*, 5246.
[162] *Jāmiʿ al-Tirmidhī*, 2799.
[163] *Ṣaḥīḥ Muslim*, 223.

"And Allah loves those who purify themselves."[164]

These two sentences alone should be enough to convince those whose hearts are open to the Truth. A woman should know the basics of cleanliness. She should know the rulings regarding her menstruation impeccably and be extremely careful with regards to cleanliness from blood and urine. She should know when and how to wash herself properly to ensure her *istinjā'*, *wuḍū*, and *ghusl* are all correct. For example, she should know never to use her right hand for *istinjā'*, but to begin on the right when washing her body. Umm al-Mu'minīn Sayyidah 'Ā'ishah ؓ said, *"The Prophet ﷺ used to like to start from the right side on wearing shoes, combing his hair and cleaning or washing himself and on doing anything else."*[165]

A woman should endeavour to look presentable to her family members and look her best for her husband. There is no harm in her dressing up for her husband either within the house or specifically in the bedroom. Such actions build closeness between spouses and ensure a healthy marriage. Dressing up for the sake of others (for '*yourself*') should, however, be avoided, as should buying excessive clothing to wear and dispose of after one outing, as this is wastefulness. Even if clothing is damaged, a woman should be able and willing to repair it, thus extending its usability and protecting her from falling into the sin of wastefulness.

Returning to the subject matter, her private parts should be shaven clean and she should keep her hair well-combed and groomed. There should be no foul odour coming from her, and so scentless deodorants are encouraged and wearing scents in the house is allowed.

Sayyidunā Abū Hurayrah ؓ narrated that Allah's Messenger ﷺ said:

---

[164] Qur'an, 9:108.
[165] *Ṣaḥīḥ al-Bukhārī*, 168.

طِيبُ الرِّجَالِ مَا ظَهَرَ رِيحُهُ وَخَفِيَ لَوْنُهُ وَطِيبُ النِّسَاءِ مَا ظَهَرَ لَوْنُهُ وَخَفِيَ رِيحُهُ

"Men's perfume is scented and colourless; women's perfume is scentless and colourful."[166]

If women wear any fragrance outside of the house, it must be very subtle and light, so as not to attract the attention of unrelated men. Inside the house, a woman can in fact wear whatever fragrance she wishes to wear, as these fragrances are intended to build attraction between her husband and her.

Lastly, psychological self-care deserves separate mention. Though men and women in the modern age are quite proficient in caring for their physical well-being and appearance, mental health issues have skyrocketed in the West. Dear sister, take care with regard to your own mental well-being and ensure that you are mentally strong within yourself. Comparing yourself to 'influencers' and the scripted lives they display online is a path to disaster, as is comparing your beauty to the edited and artificial 'models' plastered on billboards and magazines. Islam is our way of life, not the American Dream. Buying products will not bring any of us true happiness, for only complete submission to Allah will. If you are struggling, seek help first and foremost from Allah, then take steps yourself to ensure your own contentment through both prayer and action. If you must compare yourself to others, compare yourself to the pious people around you and strive to be a better bondswoman of Allah. Look to the Ṣaḥābiyāt ﵃ as your role models. Every person that exists, ever existed, or will exist was created by Allah, and is thus exactly as they should be, physically just as Allah made them. There is nothing *wrong* with how Allah has made you, and He has not created anyone more correctly than anyone else. Hold to that thought; let it strengthen you and heal the scars you have carved into your own psyche.

---

[166] *Jāmiʿ al-Tirmidhī*, 2787.

In the end, our physical forms are simply the vessels that Allah has placed us in for a short time. We are merely borrowing them and will one day return them to the earth from which they were fashioned. Beautify your soul, for this is the part of you that matters.

26
She has *Ghayrah*

عن أَسْمَاء بِنْت يَزِيد أَنَّهَا كَانَتْ عِنْدَ رَسُولِ اللَّهِ صَلَّى اللَّهُ عَلَيْهِ وَسَلَّمَ وَالرِّجَالُ وَالنِّسَاءُ
قُعُودٌ عِنْدَهُ فَقَالَ لَعَلَّ رَجُلًا يَقُولُ مَا يَفْعَلُ بِأَهْلِهِ وَلَعَلَّ امْرَأَةً تُخْبِرُ بِمَا فَعَلَتْ مَعَ زَوْجِهَا فَأَرَمَّ
الْقَوْمُ فَقُلْتُ إِي وَاللَّهِ يَا رَسُولَ اللَّهِ إِنَّهُنَّ لَيَقُلْنَ وَإِنَّهُمْ لَيَفْعَلُونَ قَالَ فَلَا تَفْعَلُوا فَإِنَّمَا ذَلِكَ مِثْلُ
الشَّيْطَانِ لَقِيَ شَيْطَانَةً فِي طَرِيقٍ فَغَشِيَهَا وَالنَّاسُ يَنْظُرُونَ

Asmā' bint Yazīd narrated that she was with Allah's Messenger ﷺ while men and women were sitting with him. The Prophet ﷺ said, "Perhaps a man will say what he did in his house? Perhaps a woman will tell what she did with her husband?" The people sat in silent embarrassment, so I said, "By Allah, the women say so and the men do so." The Prophet ﷺ said, "Do not do so. Indeed it is like male and female devils fornicating in the street while people look on."[167]

Moral virtue is a key quality for men and women alike, especially for the believers. Moral virtue is understanding right from wrong and living by a code that ensures that one is always in the right. The hypothetical example of the Prophet ﷺ shows that lapses in moral virtue can be catastrophic. A minor breach of one's moral code can be akin to a major breach. Men and women speaking freely with each other about matters which should remain between spouses is akin to open fornication, because though the physical act is not being carried out, the immodesty of the act is being shared between two unmarried people. Every part of our bodies can fall into adultery and sin, and our tongues and ears are no different from our eyes and hands in this regard. Sayyidunā Abū Hurayrah ؓ narrates that Allah's Messenger ﷺ said,

الْعَيْنَانِ زِنَاهُمَا النَّظَرُ وَالأُذُنَانِ زِنَاهُمَا الإِسْتِمَاعُ وَاللِّسَانُ زِنَاهُ الْكَلَامُ وَالْيَدُ زِنَاهَا
الْبَطْشُ وَالرِّجْلُ زِنَاهَا الْخُطَا وَالْقَلْبُ يَهْوَى وَيَتَمَنَّى وَيُصَدِّقُ ذَلِكَ الْفَرْجُ وَيُكَذِّبُهُ

---

[167] *Musnad al-Imām Aḥmad*, 27036.

"The adultery of the eyes is the lustful look; the adultery of the ears is listening to lustful words; the adultery of the tongue is licentious speech; the adultery of the hand is the lustful embrace; and the adultery of the feet is to walk where one may err. The heart yearns and desires and one may realise its desires or reject them."[168]

Morality must dictate how we act in any given situation. Where it is black and white, a woman must keep herself far from the border lest she slip and find herself on the wrong side; where it is grey, she must tread more carefully still, avoiding those areas entirely if possible. A person of morality and virtue has value; the one who is devoid of these things is worthless.

Not only must she protect herself from slipping into sin, but she must also avoid creating the opportunities and conditions for others to do so. Sayyidunā Abū Hurayrah ﵁ narrates that Allah's Messenger ﷺ said,

خَيْرُ صُفُوفِ الرِّجَالِ أَوَّلُهَا وَشَرُّهَا آخِرُهَا وَخَيْرُ صُفُوفِ النِّسَاءِ آخِرُهَا وَشَرُّهَا أَوَّلُهَا

"The best rows for men are the first rows and the worst are the last rows and the best rows for women are the last rows and the worst are the first rows."[169]

Even in *prayer*, in the mosque, caution is key. Were women to pray in front of the men, the eyes of men would stray; were they to pray amongst the men, the results would be far worse. Here, the feminists will try to shift blame, saying that men should control their gazes and that women are being 'punished' for men's lack of control. To this, we say that men *are* told to keep their gazes lowered, but Islam is not designed for the perfect human being but for humans as they are to strive for perfection. Though some men will not need to be prevented from staring at women as they walk by, many will. Men and women have both been given rules to follow that have been set by Allah and His Prophet ﷺ to ensure the healthiest society. The rules do not target

---

[168] *Ṣaḥīḥ Muslim*, 2658a.

[169] *Ṣaḥīḥ Muslim*, 440.

one gender or another, but apply to both to ensure virtuosity across both inter-gender and intra-gender relationships. Sayyidunā Abū Saʿīd al-Khudrī ؓ reported that Allah's Messenger ﷺ said,

لَا يَنْظُرُ الرَّجُلُ إِلَى عَوْرَةِ الرَّجُلِ وَلَا الْمَرْأَةُ إِلَى عَوْرَةِ الْمَرْأَةِ وَلَا يُفْضِي الرَّجُلُ إِلَى الرَّجُلِ فِي ثَوْبٍ وَاحِدٍ وَلَا تُفْضِي الْمَرْأَةُ إِلَى الْمَرْأَةِ فِي الثَّوْبِ الْوَاحِدِ

> "A man should not look at the private parts of another man, nor should a woman look at the private parts of another woman.[170] A man should not lie with another man under a single blanket, nor should a woman lie with another woman under a single blanket."[71]

One's chastity must be protected with extreme jealousy to ensure that mistakes are not made and sins are not committed. Even with members of the same sex (as we have already discussed) one should remain vigilant and free of blame. In today's broken society, it is all the more important to follow these rules.

A woman should have *ghayrah* for her feminine honour – that which gives her status in society as a chaste and moral person. The word *'ghayrah'* has no equivalent in the western world, which explains why it is so rarely found here. To explain *'ghayrah'* in English requires some time. *Ghayrah* is a form of protective jealousy or vigilant protectiveness over something that is rightly yours. This can be tangible, such as property, or something intangible, such as relationships, rights, or ideas. It is a feeling of honour or respect which needs to be guarded. When that protection is broken, or lines are crossed, the ones affected feel a sense of affront. It is an earnest concern felt over things that matter and are dear to you, such as your land, your spouse, your children, your honour, or your self-respect. A woman who has *ghayrah* has the highest morals and is modest in dress,

---

[170] Though western readers unfamiliar with Islamic modesty may understand the 'private parts' to be the genitals, this is not necessarily the case. The man's private area is from above the navel to below the knees, and the woman's private area is *at least* her entire body excluding her face, hands below the wrist, and feet below the ankles, if not her entire body (including her voice).
[171] *Ṣaḥīḥ Muslim*, 338.

words, and actions. She is mindful of keeping herself away from anything which could bring her honour into question. If one has *ghayrah*, she should not be able to stand for immodesty in any form, nor allow it to be associated with her and those she holds most dear.

Umm al-Mu'minīn Sayyidah ʿĀ'ishah ؓ narrated that Allah's Messenger ﷺ said,

يَا أُمَّةَ مُحَمَّدٍ مَا أَحَدٌ أَغْيَرَ مِنَ اللَّهِ أَنْ يَرَى عَبْدَهُ أَوْ أَمَتَهُ تَزْنِي يَا أُمَّةَ مُحَمَّدٍ لَوْ تَعْلَمُونَ مَا أَعْلَمُ لَضَحِكْتُمْ قَلِيلاً وَلَبَكَيْتُمْ كَثِيرًا.

"O followers of Muhammad! There is none, who has more ghayrah than Allah, so He has forbidden that His slave fornicates or His slave girl fornicates. O followers of Muhammad! If you only knew what I know, you would laugh less and weep more!"[172]

---

[172] *Ṣaḥīḥ al-Bukhārī*, 5221.

27

She has *Ḥayā'*

عَنْ أَسْمَاءَ بِنْتِ أَبِي بَكْرٍ ـ رضى الله عنهما ـ قَالَتْ:

تَزَوَّجَنِي الزُّبَيْرُ، وَمَا لَهُ فِي الأَرْضِ مِنْ مَالٍ، وَلاَ مَمْلُوكٍ، وَلاَ شَىْءٍ غَيْرَ نَاضِحٍ، وَغَيْرَ فَرَسِهِ، فَكُنْتُ أَعْلِفُ فَرَسَهُ، وَأَسْتَقِي الْمَاءَ، وَأَخْرِزُ غَرْبَهُ وَأَعْجِنُ، وَلَمْ أَكُنْ أُحْسِنُ أَخْبِزُ، وَكَانَ يَخْبِزُ جَارَاتٌ لِي مِنَ الأَنْصَارِ وَكُنَّ نِسْوَةَ صِدْقٍ، وَكُنْتُ أَنْقُلُ النَّوَى مِنْ أَرْضِ الزُّبَيْرِ الَّتِي أَقْطَعَهُ رَسُولُ اللَّهِ صلى الله عليه وسلم عَلَى رَأْسِي، وَهْىَ مِنِّي عَلَى ثُلُثَىْ فَرْسَخٍ. فَجِئْتُ يَوْمًا وَالنَّوَى عَلَى رَأْسِي فَلَقِيتُ رَسُولَ اللَّهِ صلى الله عليه وسلم وَمَعَهُ نَفَرٌ مِنَ الأَنْصَارِ فَدَعَانِي ثُمَّ قَالَ إِخْ إِخْ. لِيَحْمِلَنِي خَلْفَهُ، فَاسْتَحْيَيْتُ أَنْ أَسِيرَ مَعَ الرِّجَالِ، وَذَكَرْتُ الزُّبَيْرَ وَغَيْرَتَهُ، وَكَانَ أَغْيَرَ النَّاسِ، فَعَرَفَ رَسُولُ اللَّهِ صلى الله عليه وسلم أَنِّي قَدِ اسْتَحْيَيْتُ فَمَضَى. فَجِئْتُ الزُّبَيْرَ فَقُلْتُ لَقِيَنِي رَسُولُ اللَّهِ صلى الله عليه وسلم وَعَلَى رَأْسِي النَّوَى، وَمَعَهُ نَفَرٌ مِنْ أَصْحَابِهِ، فَأَنَاخَ لأَرْكَبَ، فَاسْتَحْيَيْتُ مِنْهُ وَعَرَفْتُ غَيْرَتَكَ. فَقَالَ وَاللَّهِ لَحَمْلُكِ النَّوَى كَانَ أَشَدَّ عَلَىَّ مِنْ رُكُوبِكِ مَعَهُ. قَالَتْ حَتَّى أَرْسَلَ إِلَىَّ أَبُو بَكْرٍ بَعْدَ ذَلِكَ بِخَادِمٍ يَكْفِينِي سِيَاسَةَ الْفَرَسِ، فَكَأَنَّمَا أَعْتَقَنِي.

Asmā' bint Abū Bakr ﵄ narrates:

"When al-Zubayr married me, he had no real property, slave, or anything else except a camel which drew water from the well, and his horse. I used to feed his horse with fodder, draw water, sew the bucket for drawing it, and prepare the dough, though I did not know how to bake bread so our Anṣārī neighbours used to bake bread for me. They were honourable ladies. I used to carry the date stones on my head from al-Zubayr's land, given to him by Allah's Messenger ﷺ, and this land was two thirds of a *farsakh*[178] from my house. One day, while I was returning with date stones on my head, I met Allah's Messenger ﷺ along with some Anṣārī people. He called me and then said, 'Ikh! Ikh!' directing his camel to kneel so as to offer me a ride. I felt shy to travel with men and remembered al-Zubayr and his *ghayrah*, as he was from amongst those with the greatest sense of

[178] A unit used to measure walking distances (likely for military usage), just over three miles or five kilometres.

ghayrah. Allah's Messenger ﷺ noticed my shyness and so he proceeded on. I came to al-Zubayr and said, 'I met Allah's Messenger ﷺ while carrying date stones on my head, and he had some Ṣaḥābah with him. He made his camel kneel down so that I might ride, but I felt shy in his presence and remembered your *ghayrah*.' On that al-Zubayr said, 'By Allah, your carrying the date stones is more shameful to me than your riding with him.' I continued in this way until Abū Bakr sent me a servant to look after the horse. I felt as if he had set me free."[174]

For women, the discussion on self-value and self-respect is closely tied to the idea of *ghayrah*, which we covered in the previous section. In the above hadith, we see the *ghayrah* of Sayyidah Asmā' ؓ in full effect, fuelled in part by the *ghayrah* of her husband, Sayyidunā al-Zubayr ؓ.[175] Her sense of shyness and self-*ghayrah* was such that even when being offered a ride on the camel of Allah's Messenger ﷺ to alleviate the burden of carrying the weight of date stones on her head, she did not accept the offer. Sayyidunā Abū Hurayrah ؓ narrated that Allah's Messenger ﷺ said,

الإيمَانُ بِضْعٌ وَسِتُّونَ شُعْبَةً، وَالْحَيَاءُ شُعْبَةٌ مِنَ الإيمَانِ.

"Faith consists of more than sixty branches, and *ḥayā'* is a part of faith."[176]

The word *ḥayā'* is another word that does not have an equivalent in English, and the impact of this can again be seen in the behaviours of the people in the English-speaking world. *Ḥayā'* is bashfulness and shyness, self-respect and self-value, modesty, scruple, and moral virtue.

---

[174] *Ṣaḥīḥ al-Bukhārī*, 5224.
[175] It is worth noting that Sayyidunā al-Zubayr ؓ had no property save for his camel and his horse (which he used in military expeditions), but the daughter of the foremost Ṣaḥābī of the Prophet ﷺ, Sayyidunā Abū Bakr ؓ, married him. This shows the value that the Ṣaḥābah ؓ placed on the faith and good character of suitors for the hands of their daughters.
[176] *Ṣaḥīḥ al-Bukhārī*, 9.

A Muslimah should epitomise *ḥayā'* and guard herself from falling afoul of base influences from the outside world. The world will speak of liberation and freedom but in practice it wants only to strip away your *ḥayā'* and your modesty, so it can gaze upon you with its lustful eyes and take your honour from you with your own consent. All of this is achieved through the seeds of self-honouring and pride. Both Sayyidunā Abū Sa'īd al-Khudrī ﵁ and Sayyidunā Abū Hurayrah ﵁ reported that the Prophet ﷺ narrated that Allah has said,

الْعِزُّ إِزَارِي، وَالْكِبْرِيَاءُ رِدَائِي، فَمَنْ نَازَعَنِي بِشَيْءٍ مِنْهُمَا عَذَّبْتُهُ.

"Honour is My Garment and Pride is My Cloak. Whoever vies with Me regarding one of them, I shall punish him."[177]

The above quotation is not meant in a literal sense, but figuratively. Allah is telling us through His noble Prophet ﷺ that true Honour can only be found with Allah Alone, as all other forms of honour are bestowed by Him. None but Allah can have Pride, as all achievements are from Allah. Only Allah can truly achieve anything, as the creation is entirely reliant on Allah in every way.

Returning to the hadith in discussion, Sayyidah Asmā' ﵂ continued to work in this way until Sayyidunā Abū Bakr ﵁, her father, sent her help. She did not ask for help to fulfil her responsibilities, nor did she complain. Her duties were those expected of a wife in a Muslim household, and thus she worked hard to complete them without complaint. In her own words, these included feeding the horse with fodder, drawing water from the well, mending the bucket, carrying date stones over a two mile journey, and preparing the dough.[178] She was confident in her role and position as a woman. She knew where she

---

[177] *Al-Adab Al-Mufrad*, 552.

[178] This hadith also highlights the sisterhood of the Ṣaḥābiyāt ﵅, who would help each other with fulfilling their duties. This is how their community functioned; women helped each other and men helped each other. An Islamic community is not built through the free mixing of men and women, as Muslims in the west are starting to believe due to outside influences, but through intra-gender support and togetherness.

stood and what her value was, and carried out her duties with confidence and due diligence.

The Ṣaḥābiyāt ﷺ never had an issue with being women and what that entailed, just as their male counterparts did not complain about carrying out their own duties. Each group knew exactly what was required and did it without complaint. The Muslims of today have become obsessed with emulating non-Muslim 'influencers' and 'stars' at the expense of a superior way of living. What is it about western society that makes us think it is superior to our own? What success have they seen *as a society* that entices us into emulating them for the same alleged benefits? Is it the breakdown of the family unit? Is it the destruction of the natural understanding of what gender is? Perhaps it is the immorality and rampant sexual deviancy that makes us think 'these people are doing a great job'? Or is it merely the fear of being 'judged' by non-Muslims?

A Muslim should not fear what others may think, say, or do. If Allah has decreed that we behave in such a way, then we will do so; if the Prophet ﷺ has taught us how to live our lives in the best possible way then we will not worry about what anyone else will say.

To be, or not to be, that is the question:

Whether 'tis nobler in the mind to suffer

The slings and arrows of outrageous fortune,

Or to take arms against a sea of troubles

And by opposing end them.[179]

As women, is success really only measured against the yardstick of manhood? If you give up your children to a *kāfir* education system that teaches irreligiosity, deviant sexual immorality, gender dysphoria, and the perpetuation of this system, will you feel like you have finally achieved self-worth? Your value is not to be found in 'manning up',

[179] William Shakespeare, *Hamlet*.

nor in obeying your bosses at work while you argue with your husband at home, nor in pursuing a university education for the sake of someone in an ivory tower giving you a paper to say that you have studied. Your value is found in your adherence to Islam. Invest in your faith, perfect your good character through noble deeds, and bear the fruits of true success. You will find no happiness in the morning commute, nor in the stress of exams, nor the endless meetings and wasted time at work. Spend your day with your own children, whom you are literally designed to raise and care for, be the guardian of your household, and live your life according to the Qur'an and Sunnah. *In shā Allāh* you will taste happiness in both this life and the next.

28
She Knows Her Limits

عَنْ أَبِي هُرَيْرَةَ ـ رضى الله عنه ـ قَالَ قَالَ رَسُولُ اللَّهِ صلى الله عليه وسلم:

اسْتَوْصُوا بِالنِّسَاءِ، فَإِنَّ الْمَرْأَةَ خُلِقَتْ مِنْ ضِلَعٍ، وَإِنَّ أَعْوَجَ شَىْءٍ فِي الضِّلَعِ أَعْلاَهُ، فَإِنْ ذَهَبْتَ تُقِيمُهُ كَسَرْتَهُ، وَإِنْ تَرَكْتَهُ لَمْ يَزَلْ أَعْوَجَ، فَاسْتَوْصُوا بِالنِّسَاءِ.

Abū Hurayrah ﷺ narrated that Allah's Messenger ﷺ said:

"Be kind to women, for a woman is created from a rib. The most curved portion of the rib is its upper portion. If you try to straighten it, it will break; if you leave it as it is, it will remain crooked. So, be kind to women."[180]

This hadith is well-known amongst the masses and oft-quoted. There is a sub-group of women that becomes confused at this hadith and finds themselves almost trying to argue against it (Allah's refuge is sought). To them, we say look a little deeper at the hadith and leave your ego at the door. Allah's Messenger ﷺ advised kindness and good treatment toward women at both the beginning and the end of the hadith, reinforcing the idea that men should not mistreat the women in their care. Allah says,

خَلَقَكُم مِّن نَّفْسٍ وَٰحِدَةٍ ثُمَّ جَعَلَ مِنْهَا زَوْجَهَا

"He created you from a single soul, then from it He made its mate."[181]

The example of the rib, from which our noble mother Sayyidah Ḥawwā' ﷺ was created, is indeed an astute and nuanced example. Men are advised not to be harsh in trying to force women to behave in a manner they wish them to behave, lest the strain of this harshness breaks them; but they are also warned not to become complacent, for if they make no effort in this regard she will remain in the same state.

---

[180] *Ṣaḥīḥ al-Bukhārī*, 3331.
[181] Qur'an, 39:6.

Men, and by this we mean *real men* who abide by the Qur'an and Sunnah and exemplify true masculinity,[182] are charged with the responsibility of looking after and effectively managing their household and its dependents, which in Islamic society includes their wives. Allah says:

ٱلرِّجَالُ قَوَّٰمُونَ عَلَى ٱلنِّسَآءِ بِمَا فَضَّلَ ٱللَّهُ بَعْضَهُمْ عَلَىٰ بَعْضٍ وَبِمَآ أَنفَقُوا۟ مِنْ أَمْوَٰلِهِمْ ۚ

"Men are the caretakers of women, as men have been provisioned by Allah over women and tasked with supporting them financially."[183]

As women, Muslimahs should be aware of this and accept it for what it is, even if their hearts (too often tainted by the broken society they live in, just like their male counterparts) may not take to the idea immediately. Men and women have equitable positions in Islamic society, but not *equal* positions. Men are charged with supervisory roles within the household and with the responsibilities expected of them in any working and healthy society: protection, provision, and guidance. Women have a managerial role of the home itself and have the responsibilities that are expected of them: supporting, caring, and safekeeping. Each of us are shepherds, and each of us is responsible for our own flock. We all have limitations and a woman should be aware of her own.

Ask yourself this: if a man and a woman engaged in any sporting activity where the competitors are of equal height and weight, who is going to win? If you answered the latter, you are deluding yourself. Men are physiologically and psychologically built differently to women. This is a fact. Men naturally have more lean muscle, less body fat, denser bones, and more musculature in the required areas to be more competitive in any physical category. This is why sporting events *always* differentiate by gender. Any modern attempt to try to argue this point is sheer idiocy and delusion. Men are more competitive, more willing to do what it takes to win, more aggressive, and more able to reason by

---

[182] See *40 Hadith on Masculinity: How to be a Good Man* for further details on what this entails.
[183] Qur'an, 4:34.

logic rather than emotion. All of this is to say that men and women were created differently to specialise in certain roles and fields. Where women excel, men cannot hope to compete, and vice versa. A woman should know what her limitations are and where she is weak, not just physically, but psychologically and spiritually, and then work to improve herself in line with the Sharia.

Sayyidunā Abū Mūsā ﵁ narrates that Allah's Messenger ﷺ said,

كَمَلَ مِنْ الرِّجَالِ كَثِيرٌ وَلَمْ يَكْمُلْ مِنْ النِّسَاءِ إِلَّا آسِيَةُ امْرَأَةُ فِرْعَوْنَ وَمَرْيَمُ بِنْتُ عِمْرَانَ وَإِنَّ فَضْلَ عَائِشَةَ عَلَى النِّسَاءِ كَفَضْلِ الثَّرِيدِ عَلَى سَائِرِ الطَّعَامِ.

"There were many men who achieved perfection, but none were perfect among women but Āsiyah, the wife of Pharaoh, and Maryam, the daughter of ʿImrān. And the excellence of ʿĀʾishah above other women is as the excellence of tharīd[184] *above all other foods."*[185]

It is common these days for women to tell each other that they are perfect, and that no one should tell them that they need to improve themselves. 'You're a ten,' they say, 'You can do much better.' Ignoring the terrible advice itself that will ultimately lead to the breakdown of a marriage, this idea that any woman alive today can achieve perfection is preposterous. The Prophet ﷺ has listed the women that attained 'perfection', which according to Imam Ibn Ḥajar al-ʿAsqalānī ﵀ implies Prophethood,[186] since sainthood, truthfulness, and martyrdom are found in womenfolk in abundance.[187]

This refers to the verse:

وَمَن يُطِعِ ٱللَّهَ وَٱلرَّسُولَ فَأُو۟لَـٰٓئِكَ مَعَ ٱلَّذِينَ أَنْعَمَ ٱللَّهُ عَلَيْهِم مِّنَ ٱلنَّبِيِّـۧنَ وَٱلصِّدِّيقِينَ وَٱلشُّهَدَآءِ وَٱلصَّـٰلِحِينَ ۚ وَحَسُنَ أُو۟لَـٰٓئِكَ رَفِيقًا (٦٩)

---

[184] A bread-soup that was popular at the time.
[185] *Ṣaḥīḥ Muslim*, 2431.
[186] It should be noted here that the majority of scholars do not hold the opinion that any woman was granted Prophethood.
[187] *Fatḥ al-Bārī bi-Sharḥ Ṣaḥīḥ al-Bukhārī*, vol. 10, p. 167.

"And whoever obeys Allah and the Messenger will be in the company of those blessed by Allah: the Prophets, the people of truth, the martyrs, and the righteous – what honourable company!"[188]

Women can, and should strive to, reach the highest statuses amongst the believers, so care should be taken to understand what *is not* being said. You cannot achieve perfection, but human beings are not meant to achieve it. Only Allah is Absolutely Perfect. What is important is that you strive to achieve a status as close to perfection as possible and in so doing become the best version of yourself.

With these matters fully in perspective, we can now move onto the final point in this section in that the hadith also highlights positive qualities that good women should try to build within themselves: flexibility and adaptiveness. It is a natural inclination to be defensive and stubborn when others seek to change, as the hadith clearly implies, but a woman that can learn to be flexible in her behaviour and adapt to her situation has the prerequisites to succeed both in this life and the next. When a woman marries, she must leave her home environment and enter into the care of a man, who she may not know at all. His lifestyle may differ to hers, and his wider family may operate differently to hers. She must be able to adapt, be flexible, and compromise on matters. Failure to do so results in a failure of marriage. This is not to say that she gives up on her Islamic principles: where Allah and His Messenger ﷺ are concerned, no husband's lifestyle or preferences can ever compete. Though here, we would also add that she should ensure that such an issue never rears itself up *by selecting the right partner in the first place.*

---

[188] Qur'an, 4:69.

29
She Hones Her Mind

عَنْ صَفِيَّةَ بِنْتِ شَيْبَةَ قَالَتْ عَائِشَةُ رضي الله عنها:

نِعْمَ النِّسَاءُ نِسَاءُ الأَنْصَارِ لَمْ يَكُنْ يَمْنَعُهُنَّ الْحَيَاءُ أَنْ يَتَفَقَّهْنَ فِي الدِّينِ.

وفي رواية أخرى قالت: لَمْ يَكُنْ يَمْنَعُهُنَّ الْحَيَاءُ أَنْ يَسْأَلْنَ عَنِ الدِّينِ وَيَتَفَقَّهْنَ فِيهِ

Ṣafiyyah bint Shaybah narrated that ʿĀ'ishah ﷺ said:

"How excellent are the women of the Anṣār! They do not allow shyness to prevent them from understanding the Faith."

In another narration, she ﷺ said, "They do not allow shyness to prevent them from asking questions about the Faith and understanding it."[189]

A woman gathers wisdom, knowledge, and understanding as she grows, knowing that she will never be the finished article. She will grow as she experiences life and gain understanding from its journey. Sayyidunā Abū Saʿīd ﷺ narrated that Allah's Messenger ﷺ said,

لاَ حَلِيمَ إِلاَّ ذُو عَثْرَةٍ وَلاَ حَكِيمَ إِلاَّ ذُو تَجْرِبَةٍ.

"There is no forbearance except for the one who has stumbled, and there is no wisdom except for the one who has experienced."[190]

Knowledge is an ocean; we can take as much as we can carry from this ocean every day for the rest of our lives and there will always be more to learn. A good woman accepts this and takes solace in the vastness of it for she will never run out of things to learn, skills to master, and ways to better herself.

There are no restrictions on learning, and there is no such thing as useless knowledge – it will always be useful to someone, somewhere. Knowing every major clothing brand, the names of their designers,

---

[189] *Ṣaḥīḥ Muslim*, 332.
[190] *Jāmiʿ al-Tirmidhī*, 2033.

their logo history, and the products that set them apart has no use for the common woman, but to someone in the field, such as a competitor, such information is invaluable. A person that is not the manager of a football team does not need to know the names of every professional player in the local league along with their merits and weaknesses, but a manager is required to have this information to do his job. Individual fields of knowledge can also be ranked according to their universal value. Languages and mathematics are indispensable forms of knowledge and, to a lesser extent, so are the natural sciences. Knowledge of poetry or art, though it is important for some people to understand them too, is less so. Chief among all forms of knowledge are those fields that relate to the religion of Islam. Even within these fields there is a hierarchy.

In short, it should suffice us to say that *some forms of knowledge are more beneficial than others, and some forms of knowledge are only beneficial to some.*

First and foremost, as a Muslim woman, one should learn the basics of the Faith. This is key. All other forms of knowledge should be set aside prior to gaining a good understanding of the core of Islam. One's beliefs, the types and methods of worship, knowing halal and haram, understanding the basic *fiqh* that one needs to employ to live her daily life – these are fields of knowledge that take a woman years to learn and a lifetime to master. As mentioned previously, a woman (and her guardian) should choose the right spouse when getting married, as she should primarily seek this knowledge from the books of established scholars and expect her husband to teach her from these books. If he is lacking here, then it is best for both people to learn together. Should there be a necessity to go out to learn, there is no harm in this *per se* but it should not be one's default choice. The default position should always be where there is most safety, and thus learning from home will always be the preference. With the advent of online learning, a woman can access female teachers from the comfort of her home. There is no requirement for her to attend so-called Islamic talks where the genders are mixed and the male speakers have direct line of sight with the women in attendance (and vice versa), as this is far from 'Islamic'. If you feel an objection rising, ask yourself this: is it okay for a man to attend a young female speaker's talk for the sake of Islamic reminders? Hopefully, you answered 'no'. It is *not* okay.

Take the following hadith for an example. Umm al-Mu'minīn Sayyidah Ḥafṣah ﵂ narrated:

قَالَ رَسُولُ اللهِ صَلَّى اللهُ عَلَيْهِ وَسَلَّمَ: إِنِّي لَأَرْجُو أَنْ لَا يَدْخُلَ النَّارَ، إِنْ شَاءَ اللهُ، أَحَدٌ شَهِدَ بَدْرًا، وَالْحُدَيْبِيَةَ. قَالَتْ: فَقُلْتُ أَلَيْسَ اللهُ عَزَّ وَجَلَّ يَقُولُ: 'وَإِنْ مِنْكُمْ إِلَّا وَارِدُهَا'؟ قَالَتْ: فَسَمِعْتُهُ يَقُولُ: 'ثُمَّ نُنَجِّي الَّذِينَ اتَّقَوْا وَنَذَرُ الظَّالِمِينَ فِيهَا جِثِيًّا'.

"Allah's Messenger ﷺ said, 'In shā Allāh, I hope that no one who witnessed Badr or Ḥudaybiyah will enter the Fire.' I said, 'Does Allah, the Mighty and Sublime, not say: "There is none of you who will not pass over it"?'[191]

'Then We will deliver those who were devout, leaving the wrongdoers there on their knees,'[192] *he replied."*[193]

Umm al-Mu'minīn Sayyidah Ḥafṣah ﵂ learned the religion from Allah's Messenger ﷺ himself. She had a knowledgeable father, and knowledgeable friends and relatives she could have sought other knowledge from, but her husband was the '*House of Wisdom*'[194] and so she remained at home and learned from him. She attained a deep understanding of the religion by focusing her sharp mind on gathering as much Islamic knowledge as possible and asking questions, and as a result continued to grow in wisdom, knowledge, and understanding. The wives of the Prophet ﷺ were studious women of intuition and had a great capacity and yearning for knowledge. They were chosen by Allah to be the wives of the Prophet ﷺ and through them we have received vast amounts of information around how the Prophet ﷺ was

---

[191] Qur'an, 19:71.
[192] Qur'an, 19:72.
[193] *Musnad al-Imām Aḥmad,* 26440.
[194] *Jāmiʿ al-Tirmidhī*, 3723.

in his home, as well as literally thousands of hadith texts covering a wide array of fields. Their societal contribution was not made by them going out and working, nor by leaving him to study one field or another. They contributed by obeying the Commands of Allah and His Messenger ﷺ.

A Muslimah needs to know the basics of the Faith so she can impart it upon the children of the household. It is a necessity for her. In most cases, what is not a necessity is to go out seeking university education for the sake of having a degree or entering into the workforce. Of course, if she has no other means of looking after herself and her children then there is no harm in this. It says more about the state of Muslim society than her if she is forced to take on the responsibilities of a man to make ends meet.

30
She is Organised

عَنْ يَعْلَى بْنِ مَمْلَكٍ أَنَّهُ سَأَلَ أُمَّ سَلَمَةَ زَوْجَ النَّبِيِّ صَلَّى اللَّهُ عَلَيْهِ وَسَلَّمَ عَنْ قِرَاءَةِ النَّبِيِّ صَلَّى اللَّهُ عَلَيْهِ وَسَلَّمَ وَصَلَاتِهِ فَقَالَتْ:

مَا لَكُمْ وَصَلَاتَهُ كَانَ يُصَلِّي ثُمَّ يَنَامُ قَدْرَ مَا صَلَّى ثُمَّ يُصَلِّي قَدْرَ مَا نَامَ ثُمَّ يَنَامُ قَدْرَ مَا صَلَّى حَتَّى يُصْبِحَ ثُمَّ نَعَتَتْ قِرَاءَتَهُ فَإِذَا هِيَ تَنْعَتُ قِرَاءَةً مُفَسَّرَةً حَرْفًا حَرْفًا.

Yaʿlā ibn Mamlak narrated that he asked the wife of the Prophet ﷺ, Umm Salamah, about the recitation of the Prophet ﷺ and his prayer. Umm Salamah said:

"His prayer was not as you can pray. He would pray and then sleep for as long as he prayed, then pray the amount he slept, and then sleep the amount he prayed, until the morning came. His recitation was distinct, letter for letter."[195]

A Muslimah should seek to emulate the routine lifestyle that Umm al-Mu'minīn Sayyidah Umm Salamah ﵂ described in the above hadith. Not only in prayer, but in all her dealings. Organisation requires prior planning and preparation, and the establishment of a routine. Routines allow time-management to flow easier and, when followed diligently, lead to punctuality and consistently good returns. Organisation and time-management allow us to create the conditions for optimal performance in everything we do. Whether someone is arranging the logistics for the running of a school or ensuring she has enough sleep prior to Fajr so she can prepare her children's breakfast in the morning, these skills are indispensable. The Prophet ﷺ allotted a specific time for everything, ensuring that his duties as the Final Prophet of Allah ﷻ were fulfilled whilst allocating time to help people that came to him and for spending time with his wives and children.

Umm al-Mu'minīn Sayyidah ʿĀ'ishah ﵂ narrated:

---

[195] *Jāmiʿ al-Tirmidhī*, 2923.

أَنَّ النَّبِيَّ صَلَّى اللهُ عَلَيْهِ وَسَلَّمَ بَعَثَ إِلَى عُثْمَانَ بْنِ مَظْعُونٍ فَجَاءَهُ فَقَالَ يَا عُثْمَانُ أَرَغِبْتَ عَنْ سُنَّتِي؟ قَالَ لَا وَاللهِ يَا رَسُولَ اللهِ وَلَكِنْ سُنَّتَكَ أَطْلُبُ. قَالَ فَإِنِّي أَنَامُ وَأُصَلِّي وَأَصُومُ وَأُفْطِرُ وَأَنْكِحُ النِّسَاءَ فَاتَّقِ اللهَ يَا عُثْمَانُ فَإِنَّ لِأَهْلِكَ عَلَيْكَ حَقًّا وَإِنَّ لِضَيْفِكَ عَلَيْكَ حَقًّا وَإِنَّ لِنَفْسِكَ عَلَيْكَ حَقًّا فَصُمْ وَأَفْطِرْ وَصَلِّ وَنَمْ.

"The Prophet ﷺ sent for 'Uthmān ibn Maẓ'ūn and he came to him. The Prophet ﷺ said, "Uthmān, do you reject my Sunnah?" 'Uthmān said, 'No, by Allah! O Allah's Messenger, I seek your Sunnah.' The Prophet ﷺ said, 'Indeed, I sleep and I pray, I fast and I break my fast, and I marry women. Be mindful of Allah, 'Uthmān, for your family has rights over you and your guest has rights over you. Indeed, your self has rights over you. So, fast and break your fast, pray and sleep.'"[196]

A woman should ensure her time is correctly divided across the things that matter most. Time for worship should be placed at the forefront of any such scheduling, and all other duties built around this. Her children have a right upon her, her husband has his right, her parents have a right, as do her duties and, importantly, herself. Time is the great currency of our lives. It cannot be added to, it is spent whether we wish to use it or not, and it is finite. It *ends*. Sayyidunā Ibn 'Abbās ؓ narrates that Allah's Messenger ﷺ said,

اغْتَنِمْ خَمْسًا قَبْلَ خَمْسٍ شَبَابَكَ قَبْلَ هَرَمِكَ وَصِحَّتَكَ قَبْلَ سَقَمِكَ وَغِنَاكَ قَبْلَ فَقْرِكَ وَفَرَاغَكَ قَبْلَ شُغْلِكَ وَحَيَاتَكَ قَبْلَ مَوْتِكَ

"Take advantage of five before five: your youth before your old age, your health before your illness, your wealth before your poverty, your free time before your occupation, and your life before your death."[197]

In another hadith, Sayyidunā Ibn 'Abbās ؓ narrated that Allah's Messenger ﷺ said,

---

[196] *Sunan Abī Dāwūd*, 1369.
[197] Abū Bakr Aḥmad ibn al-Ḥusayn al-Bayhaqī, *Shu'ab al-Īmān*, 10250.

نِعْمَتَانِ مَغْبُونٌ فِيهِمَا كَثِيرٌ مِنَ النَّاسِ الصِّحَّةُ وَالْفَرَاغُ.

"Two blessings are often squandered by many: good health and free time."[198]

Manage your time correctly, and be punctual in the parameters and schedules you set yourself. Be diligent and do not waste your time in frivolous pursuits. Too often we waste entire days binge-watching television shows, playing video games, and scrolling endlessly through social media. Set a routine of worship and build your day around it. Ensure your duties are fulfilled and the people in your care are given some of your time and undivided attention. Be organised and plan properly, so you can create windows of time for yourself and your own well-being. We must capitalise upon the advantages we have in the here and now, and we must act in our best interests whilst we have the chance. For when we are old, we lack energy; when we are ill, we lack strength; when we are poor, we lack resources; when we are busy, we lack opportunity; and when we are dead, our books will be closed. When our books are closed, we will lament the time we wasted and say, 'Would that I had invested my time and exchanged it for good deeds.'

يَقُولُ يَـٰلَيْتَنِى قَدَّمْتُ لِحَيَاتِى (٢٤)

"They will cry, 'I wish I had sent forth (something good) for my life.'"[199]

[198] *Sunan Ibn Mājah*, 4170.

[199] Qur'an, 89:24.

4 | The Mindful Woman

31
Her Faith is in Allah Alone

عَنْ عَائِشَةَ قَالَتْ قَالَ رَسُولُ اللهِ صَلَّى اللهُ عَلَيْهِ وَسَلَّمَ:

لا يُغْنِي حَذَرٌ مِنْ قَدَرٍ وَالدُّعَاءُ يَنْفَعُ مِمَّا نَزَلَ وَمَا لَمْ يَنْزِلْ وَإِنَّ الدُّعَاءَ لَيَلْقَى الْبَلاءَ فَيَعْتَلِجَانِ إِلَى يَوْمِ الْقِيَامَةِ

ʿĀ'ishah narrated that Allah's Messenger ﷺ said:

"No worldly precaution will suffice against Providence, while supplication benefits in what is sent down and what is not. Indeed a supplication will confront a trial and they will battle until the Day of Resurrection."[200]

We have come at last to the discussions on the most important relationship of all: our relationship to Allah. Our faith in Him must be absolute. This is the sign of a true believer. Each day we reaffirm this faith and our complete reliance upon Him in our prayers. We recite:

إِيَّاكَ نَعْبُدُ وَإِيَّاكَ نَسْتَعِينُ (٤)

"You we worship and You we ask for help."[201]

We seek no aid from others, only that of Allah. Our hearts are filled with devotion to Him Alone; there is no room for another. We

[200] *Al-Muʿjam al-Awsaṭ*, 2568.
[201] Qur'an, 1:4.

worship only Him. Once this firmness of belief is established in our very souls, the words of the Prophet ﷺ will have their full effect. There is no help against the Divine Decree of Allah except through Allah Alone. We can set as many contingencies as we wish to guard ourselves against all manners of trials and threats, but when our fate is written, when destiny arrives, there is nothing we can do against it except ask for help from the One Who has set destiny in motion. A Muslimah understands this completely and has internalised this reliance on Allah.

In the modern world, you will come across many trials, none greater than the attempts of the atheistic secular world to confuse you and shake your faith. They will challenge your belief with one theory after another, whether that is evolution, the Big Bang, or something else. They will do away with logic and use 'science' to attempt to move your position ever so slightly, whilst often themselves being unaware that science is but a mechanism by which things are learned, not a cause in and of itself. Umm al-Mu'minīn Sayyidah 'Ā'ishah narrated that Allah's Messenger ﷺ said,

إِنَّ أَحَدَكُمْ يَأْتِيهِ الشَّيْطَانُ فَيَقُولُ مَنْ خَلَقَكَ؟ فَيَقُولُ اللهُ. فَيَقُولُ فَمَنْ خَلَقَ اللهَ؟ فَإِذَا وَجَدَ ذَلِكَ أَحَدُكُمْ فَلْيَقْرَأْ: "آمَنْتُ بِاللهِ وَرُسُلِهِ" فَإِنَّ ذَلِكَ يُذْهِبُ عَنْهُ.

"One of you is confronted by Shayṭān, who asks, 'Who created you?' He replies, 'Allah.' Shayṭān then asks, 'Who created Allah?' If one of you finds himself in that situation, let him recite, 'I have faith in Allah and His Messengers.' This will remove it from him."[202]

We are living in such a time now. Our response should always be to reaffirm our faith in Allah and what His Messengers have brought from Him to guide us. No one should be able to shake our faith in Allah. Establishing the five prayers and their supporting supererogatory prayers, constantly remembering Allah, making supplications to Him throughout the day, and seeking His forgiveness are all ways to fortify

[202] *Musnad al-Imām Aḥmad*, 26203.

our faith, ensuring that its roots take hold in our hearts. Umm al-Mu'minīn Sayyidah ʿĀ'ishah ﵂ narrated:

دَخَلَ رَسُولُ اللهِ صَلَّى اللهُ عَلَيْهِ وَسَلَّمَ الْكَعْبَةَ مَا خَلَّفَ بَصَرُهُ مَوْضِعَ سُجُودِهِ حَتَّى خَرَجَ مِنْهَا

"Allah's Messenger ﷺ entered the Kaʿbah and his gaze did not divert from his place of prostration until he exited."[203]

This is the type of laser-focused worshipfulness we should be seeking to emulate. It cannot, however, be merely a repetition of actions. We must understand what is being said in our prayers, and wholeheartedly believe every word. Sayyidah Asmā' bint Abū Bakr ﵄ narrated that Allah's Messenger ﷺ said,

أُوحِيَ إِلَيَّ أَنَّكُمْ تُفْتَنُونَ فِي الْقُبُورِ قَرِيبًا مِنْ فِتْنَةِ الدَّجَّالِ. فَأَمَّا الْمُؤْمِنُ أَوِ الْمُسْلِمُ فَيَقُولُ مُحَمَّدٌ جَاءَنَا بِالْبَيِّنَاتِ فَأَجَبْنَا وَآمَنَّا. فَيُقَالُ نَمْ صَالِحًا عَلِمْنَا أَنَّكَ مُوقِنٌ. وَأَمَّا الْمُنَافِقُ أَوِ الْمُرْتَابُ فَيَقُولُ لاَ أَدْرِي سَمِعْتُ النَّاسَ يَقُولُونَ شَيْئًا فَقُلْتُهُ.

"It has been revealed to me that you will be tested in the grave, similar to the test of the Dajjāl. The Mu'min or the Muslim will say, 'Muhammad came to us with clear evidence and we accepted and believed in him.' It will be said, 'Rest in peace, for we know your conviction.' As for the hypocrite or the doubter, he will say, 'I do not know. I heard people saying something and I repeated it.'"[204]

Faith in Allah is more than a feeling one has. It is knowing that He controls all things, that He is ever watching, and that if you call out to Him with conviction He will answer. We are not people of ritual for the sake of ritual and barren of devotion, nor are we a people who forsake our duty and rituals entirely in the name of 'loving God' in a 'less formalised' way; these are the ways of unbelievers. We fulfil our duties, we carry out our daily acts of worship, and we do so cognisant of Allah, with the deepest devotion to Him. This faith must be made unshakeable, and it must be complete. One of history's finest examples

---

[203] *Al-Sunan al-Kubrā*, 9726.

[204] *Ṣaḥīḥ al-Bukhārī*, 7287.

of this is that of Sayyidah Sumayyah ؓ, the first martyr. Sayyidunā ʿAbdullāh ibn Masʿūd ؓ narrated:

> أَوَّلُ مَنْ أَظْهَرَ إِسْلَامَهُ رَسُولُ اللَّهِ ﷺ وَأَبُو بَكْرٍ وَعَمَّارٌ وَأُمُّهُ سُمَيَّةُ وَصُهَيْبٌ وَبِلَالٌ وَالمِقْدَادُ.

"The first to reveal their Islam were Allah's Messenger ﷺ, Abū Bakr, ʿAmmār and his mother Sumayyah, Ṣuhayb, Bilāl, and al-Miqdād."[205]

She was among the first to publicly declare her Islam, despite not having the protection of any tribe. In Arab society during the Age of Ignorance, a person was safe from harm only so long as he was under the care of a tribe or person of influence in the area. Her husband, Sayyidunā Yāsir ؓ, was a foreigner from Yemen and had no family in the area, whilst she was a freed slave and without a tribe. This did not stop her from publicly declaring her Islam. Such was her faith in Allah and her absolute conviction in the truth of the message of the Prophet ﷺ. As word spread of her conversion, as well as that of both her, Sayyidunā ʿAmmār ؓ, and her husband, she was taken hostage and publicly tortured for her beliefs, day after day. Sayyidunā ʿAbdullāh ibn Masʿūd ؓ narrated:

> إِنَّ أَبَا جَهْلٍ طَعَنَ بِحَرْبَةٍ فِي فَخِذِ سُمَيَّةَ أُمِّ عَمَّارٍ حَتَّى بَلَغَتْ فَرْجَهَا فَمَاتَتْ، فَقَالَ عَمَّارٌ: يَا رَسُولَ اللَّهِ بَلَغَ مِنَّا أَوْ بَلَغَ مِنْهَا العَذَابُ كُلَّ مَبْلَغٍ. فَقَالَ رَسُولُ اللَّهِ صَلَّى اللَّهُ عَلَيْهِ وَسَلَّمَ: «صَبْرًا أَبَا اليَقْظَانِ اللَّهُمَّ لَا تُعَذِّبْ أَحَدًا مِنْ آلِ يَاسِرٍ بِالنَّارِ».

"Abū Jahl lanced a spear through the thigh of Sumayyah, ʿAmmār's mother, until it reached her private parts and she was martyred. ʿAmmār said, 'O Allah's Messenger, our torment has reached an utmost degree.'

---

[205] Abū Bakr ʿAbdullāh ibn Muhammad ibn Abī Shaybah, *Muṣannaf Ibn Abī Shaybah*, 38541.

Allah's Messenger ﷺ said, 'Patience, Abū al-Yaqẓān. O Allah, do not punish anyone from the family of Yāsir with the Fire!'"[206]

Her faith, and that of her family, was such that day after day of agonising torture and public humiliation would not shake their belief. They bore their suffering with patience until their last breaths and were rewarded with a status that could never be taken from them. No one will ever be able to take the title of 'first martyr' from Sayyidah Sumayyah ﵂. Her name will forever be linked to the ideas of martyrdom, conviction, and faith.

Her husband, Sayyidunā Yāsir ﵁, would soon follow his wife as her chaperone on her journey to Paradise and a meeting with Allah, as the second martyr in Islam. Can there be a greater example of pure faith in Allah and the truth of Islam? This is the gold standard of faith that we should all be striving for.

Hold to your faith in Allah, and be resolute in your conviction, the fulfilling of your duties, and your devotion to Him. This is the path to success. Hold firm to it and perhaps one day, *in shā Allāh,* you will find yourself standing by the side of Sayyidah Sumayyah ﵂ as she prepares to meet with her Lord.

[206] Abū ʿAmmār Yūsuf ibn ʿAbdullāh ibn ʿAbd al-Barr, *Al-Istīʿāb fī Maʿrifah al-Aṣḥāb,* vol. 4, p. 364.

32
She Intends Good

عَنْ يَحْيَى بْنِ أَبِي سُلَيْمٍ قَالَ:

رَأَيْتُ سَمْرَاءَ بِنْتَ نَهِيكٍ رضي الله عنها وَكَانَتْ قَدْ أَدْرَكَتِ النَّبِيَّ صَلَّى اللَّهُ عَلَيْهِ وَسَلَّمَ عَلَيْهَا دِرْعٌ غَلِيظٌ وَخِمَارٌ غَلِيظٌ بِيَدِهَا سَوْطٌ تُؤَدِّبُ النَّاسَ وَتَأْمُرُ بِالْمَعْرُوفِ وَتَنْهَى عَنِ الْمُنْكَرِ.

Yaḥyā ibn Abū Sulaym reported:

"I saw Samra' bint Nahik ﵂, who had met the Prophet ﷺ. She was wearing a thick robe and a thick veil, and in her hand was a whip with which she would discipline people, enjoin good, and forbid evil."[207]

One of the key qualities of the Muslims is that we enjoin good and forbid evil. Allah says:

كُنتُمْ خَيْرَ أُمَّةٍ أُخْرِجَتْ لِلنَّاسِ تَأْمُرُونَ بِٱلْمَعْرُوفِ وَتَنْهَوْنَ عَنِ ٱلْمُنكَرِ وَتُؤْمِنُونَ بِٱللَّهِ ۗ

"You are the best community ever raised for humanity – you encourage good, forbid evil, and believe in Allah."[208]

It is what differentiates us from other peoples and nations. Aside from being the Ummah of the Prophet Muhammad ﷺ, and the people of the Qur'an, we have been given the distinction over other nations to continue the prophetic task of leading people towards the Truth and steering them away from falsehood; we are charged with rectifying the moral and spiritual ailments of society. This is done by adhering to the Sharia. Those of us who move away from the Laws of Allah and His Messenger ﷺ are failing in this fundamental duty. Sayyidah Samra' bint Nahik ﵂ was a Ṣaḥabiyah of the Prophet ﷺ. She had seen him and benefitted from his guidance directly, and thus she upheld the laws

---

[207] Sulaymān ibn Aḥmad ibn Ayyūb ibn Muṭayyir al-Ṭabarānī, *Al-Mu'jam al-Kabīr*, 785.

[208] Qur'an, 3:110.

of the Sharia. It should be noted that she wore thick clothing and fully covered and veiled herself in strict adherence to the Sharia. This was the practice of the first generation of Muslims. The hadith also states that she kept a whip, or scourge, with her to discipline the people, forbidding evil and encouraging people to do good. The Prophet ﷺ said,

مَنْ رَأَى مِنْكُمْ مُنْكَرًا فَلْيُغَيِّرْهُ بِيَدِهِ فَإِنْ لَمْ يَسْتَطِعْ فَبِلِسَانِهِ فَإِنْ لَمْ يَسْتَطِعْ فَبِقَلْبِهِ وَذَلِكَ أَضْعَفُ الإِيمَانِ.

"Whosoever amongst you witnesses evil should change it with the help of his hand; if he lacks the strength to do so, then he should change it with his tongue; if he lacks the strength enough to do so, then he should abhor it in his heart. And that is the weakest of faith."[209]

Sayyidah Samra' bint Nahīk ؓ was a Ṣaḥābiyah, and therefore she could only ever have the highest form of faith. As a Muslimah, this is the example that you should be following: strict adherence to the rules of Islam, actively encouraging one's sisters to do the same, and physically preventing them from transgressing against the Laws of Allah.

All of this should come from a place of good intention and well-wishing. No hatefulness, disdain, or spitefulness should enter a woman's heart when she sees others overtly less adherent to the Qur'an and Sunnah. Her intention should always be pure, for it just might be the case that the one she is belittling has a higher rank with Allah. The Prophet ﷺ said,

إِنَّمَا الْأَعْمَالُ بِالنِّيَّاتِ، وَإِنَّمَا لِكُلِّ امْرِئٍ مَا نَوَى

"Works are (judged) only by intentions, and so for everyone is only that which they intended."[210]

---

[209] Ṣaḥīḥ Muslim, 49a.
[210] Ṣaḥīḥ al-Bukhārī, 1.

Correcting others to belittle them, enjoining good to virtue-signal, engaging in religiosity for the purpose of showing off, and 'humble-bragging' will only be rewarded by what you seek from those things. People may consider you to be pious and 'on the *Dīn*' but there is no reward for such behaviour. In some cases, there may even be punishment.

Our actions must always be good, and we should keep the company of those who likewise act righteously. Sayyidunā Abū Mūsā ﵁ narrated that Allah's Messenger ﷺ said,

مَثَلُ الْجَلِيسِ الصَّالِحِ وَالسَّوْءِ كَحَامِلِ الْمِسْكِ وَنَافِخِ الْكِيرِ، فَحَامِلُ الْمِسْكِ إِمَّا أَنْ يُحْذِيَكَ، وَإِمَّا أَنْ تَبْتَاعَ مِنْهُ، وَإِمَّا أَنْ تَجِدَ مِنْهُ رِيحًا طَيِّبَةً، وَنَافِخُ الْكِيرِ إِمَّا أَنْ يُحْرِقَ ثِيَابَكَ، وَإِمَّا أَنْ تَجِدَ رِيحًا خَبِيثَةً.

"The example of a pious companion and an evil one is that of a person carrying musk and a person blowing the bellows.[211] *The one carrying musk will either gift you some, you will buy some from him, or you will take a pleasant fragrance from him. The one blowing the bellows will either burn your clothes or you will take a foul stench from him."*[212]

Good company is beneficial to you even if you do not receive any direct benefit, as whoever we spend our time with will influence our own behaviour and vice versa. In the same way, bad company will influence you negatively, even if you try to shield yourself from this influence. For example, if you have foul-mouthed friends, you will find yourself using foul language too, even when not in their company. It should never be the case that you look around and note that you are the best of your companions: this implies that either you are feeling pride in yourself, disdain for your friends, or you have realised that they are not good company. If the latter is the case, then correct them if possible. If you cannot correct them, through shyness or through

---

[211] A device used to stoke the furnace in a blacksmith's workshop.

[212] *Ṣaḥīḥ al-Bukhārī*, 5534.

their inability to take criticism (worded tactfully), then leave their company and make better friends.

When in the company of the good, we should strive to improve ourselves and our companions through sincere advice and friendly competition. As long as we ensure our intentions are clean and pure, there is no harm in competing with each other in good action. Allah says:

سَابِقُوٓاْ إِلَىٰ مَغْفِرَةٖ مِّن رَّبِّكُمْ وَجَنَّةٍ عَرْضُهَا كَعَرْضِ ٱلسَّمَآءِ وَٱلْأَرْضِ

"Compete each other in proceeding towards forgiveness from your Lord and to Paradise the width of which is like the width of the sky and the earth..."[213]

Allah has *told* us to do so, and thus, as Muslims, we should seek to compete in these two things: seeking forgiveness from Allah and to precede each other in the path to Paradise. The former shows us that there is no ego in this friendly competition; each of us are on the same path together but our success or failure will be ours alone. The latter shows us that it is good to compete with one another in goodness, so as to encourage our siblings in Islam to be better and do more.

[213] Qur'an, 57:21.

33
She is Consistent in her Worship

عَنْ عَائِشَةَ، قَالَتْ:

دَخَلَ عَلَىَّ رَسُولُ اللَّهِ صلى الله عليه وسلم وَعِنْدِي امْرَأَةٌ فَقَالَ مَنْ هَذِهِ؟ فَقُلْتُ امْرَأَةٌ لاَ تَنَامُ تُصَلِّي . قَالَ عَلَيْكُمْ مِنَ الْعَمَلِ مَا تُطِيقُونَ فَوَاللَّهِ لاَ يَمَلُّ اللَّهُ حَتَّى تَمَلُّوا. وَكَانَ أَحَبَّ الدِّينِ إِلَيْهِ مَا دَاوَمَ عَلَيْهِ صَاحِبُهُ.

ʿĀ'ishah said:

"Allah's Messenger ﷺ came to me whilst I was sitting with a woman. He asked, 'Who is this?' I said, 'A woman who does not sleep, but prays.' He said, 'Do what you are able to do. By Allah, Allah does not grow weary but you will. The religious act most pleasing to Him is the one in which the doer is consistent.'"[214]

Consistency will always surpass bursts of zeal and fervour. Each of us knows at least one part-time zealot, who has never opened a Qur'an or prayed a supererogatory prayer (in many cases the Muslims of today do not even pray their obligatory prayers) but when a special night or day arrives then they exhaust every effort in worship, spending the entire night in prayer until they drift away before the call to Fajr prayer, and turning page after page of the Qur'an until the words begin to jumble and blur. When calamity strikes, or they want something, you will find them the most devout of all the people in the world, but when living in their good times, they will be nowhere to be seen. May Allah accept their worship and grant them good company and guidance so they can become more consistent.

وَإِذَا مَسَّ ٱلْإِنسَـٰنَ ضُرٌّ دَعَا رَبَّهُۥ مُنِيبًا إِلَيْهِ ثُمَّ إِذَا خَوَّلَهُۥ نِعْمَةً مِّنْهُ نَسِىَ مَا كَانَ يَدْعُوٓا۟ إِلَيْهِ مِن قَبْلُ

[214] *Ṣaḥīḥ Muslim*, 785b.

"When one is touched with hardship, they cry out to their Lord, turning to Him. But as soon as He showers them with blessings from Him, they forget the One they had cried to earlier..."[215]

It is far superior to be consistent in one's worship. A sister who reads only a page of the Qur'an a day but reads it consistently will no doubt please Allah, for her intention is only to please Him and better herself through worship. *Worship is the goal.* She is far superior to her sister who only prays when she is in need, be that a need for solace, aid, or something else.

Regarding the above hadith, the Ṣaḥābiyah ﷺ in question was not one of those poor souls we described above. Her intention was pure and her zeal for the religion was no doubt true; she was a Ṣaḥābiyah of the Prophet ﷺ, and thus her intention and her fervour are without question. The advice of the Prophet ﷺ was not to reprimand her, but improve her worship and help her to benefit more from her prayers. Oftentimes, when the Prophet ﷺ advised the Ṣaḥābah ﷺ, he was advising the people who would be delivered the message later.

True piety is a quality that each of us as Muslims seeks to attain, and this is developed through consistency. For the common person, trying to spend our entire nights in prayer like the Ṣaḥābiyāt ﷺ will lead to tiring ourselves out. As the moral of a universal fable goes:

Slow and steady wins the race.

A person who trains consistently in the gym will, over time, become stronger and leaner; the same person could train 18 hours straight and receive nothing but rhabdomyolysis, resulting in them never training again. Self-betterment is not a race. Progressively incremental improvements in consistent worship is the Sunnah way to improve our worship of Allah, which is, after all, the purpose for which we were created.

---

[215] Qur'an, 39:8.

وَمَا خَلَقْتُ ٱلْجِنَّ وَٱلْإِنسَ إِلَّا لِيَعْبُدُونِ (٥٦)

"I did not create jinn and humans except to worship Me."[216]

Being worshipful slaves of Allah is our main purpose in life. Everything else we do is either ultimately unimportant or purely necessary. If our main goal in life is to worship Him, why is worshipping Allah so far down our list of priorities? When we pray (in many cases *if* we pray) it is something that we rush through, praying only what is necessary in terms of units, while barely completing the movements satisfactorily and reciting the words so hastily that it scarcely resembles speech. Is this how you approach anything else in life? If you go out to the park with your spouse, do you take your time and stroll or just jump in your car and drive a quick loop around the border and come home? When you sit down to eat a family meal, do you prepare it properly, sit together around the spread, and enjoy the food, or just throw the ingredients in the blender and share a smoothie instead? Why, then, is worship treated in this way? Enjoy your time conversing with Allah, take joy in the *opportunity* to draw nearer to Him. Do what you were made to do and take comfort in it.

The idea that worship is a 'private matter' that needs to be hidden away, never to be spoken about, is once again a Western concept. Increasingly we are finding that 'symbols of faith' are being banned from western countries, a move that is clearly aimed at the Muslim populations, creating a secular liberal mono-culture where faith practices are hidden away until they die out completely. This is far from our own view of the importance of faith and worship in daily life. Allah and His worship are our priorities, and thus we should prioritise Allah above all else. If our children's schools are making it hard for them to be Muslim and study, then take them out of those schools. If workplaces are restricting Muslims from being able to pray or dress modestly, then we should leave those workplaces too. No job or school (or even country for that matter) benefits you more than you benefit it.

[216] Qur'an, 51:56.

Human beings are not reliant on any of these things; we are reliant on Allah alone. Allah says:

ٱلْحَمْدُ لِلَّهِ رَبِّ ٱلْعَٰلَمِينَ (١) ٱلرَّحْمَٰنِ ٱلرَّحِيمِ (٢)

"All praise is for Allah – Lord of all worlds, the Most Compassionate, Most Merciful,"[217]

ٱللَّهُ ٱلصَّمَدُ (٢)

"Allah – the Sustainer."[218]

Allah sustains even those who reject and ridicule Him, Allah protects those who proclaim themselves the enemies of His Prophet ﷺ, so why do we fear that Allah will not sustain and protect us? Thank Allah, be grateful to Him, and beg Him for forgiveness for our shortcomings as individuals, as Muslims, and as a species. Remind each other to do so and wake each other in the dead of night to pray to Him when all else are lost in slumber. Umm al-Mu'minīn Sayyidah Umm Salamah ﵂ narrated:

أَنَّ النَّبِيَّ صَلَّى اللَّهُ عَلَيْهِ وَسَلَّمَ اسْتَيْقَظَ لَيْلَةً فَقَالَ سُبْحَانَ اللَّهِ مَاذَا أُنْزِلَ اللَّيْلَةَ مِنْ الْفِتْنَةِ مَاذَا أُنْزِلَ مِنْ الْخَزَائِنِ مَنْ يُوقِظُ صَوَاحِبَ الْحُجُرَاتِ يَا رُبَّ كَاسِيَةٍ فِي الدُّنْيَا عَارِيَةٍ فِي الْآخِرَةِ

"The Prophet ﷺ woke me up one night and said, 'Glory be to Allah! What trials has Allah sent down this night? What treasures has he sent down? Who will wake the inhabitants of these houses? Perhaps the well-dressed one in the world will be naked in the Hereafter.'"[219]

The trappings of this world are indeed only that: decorations that trap you with their glamour until you lose sight of your goal, ultimately destroying you like the sirens of Greek mythology.

---

[217] Qur'an, 1:1-2.
[218] Qur'an, 112:2.
[219] *Ṣaḥīḥ al-Bukhārī*, 1074.

Put Allah first and be consistent in His worship and you will be successful *in shā Allāh.*

34
She Reflects

عَنْ عَائِشَةَ قَالَتْ:

لَمَّا كَانَ لَيْلَةٌ مِنَ اللَّيَالِي قَالَ رَسُولُ اللَّهِ صلى الله عليه وسلم يَا عَائِشَةُ ذَرِينِي أَتَعَبَّدُ اللَّيْلَةَ لِرَبِّي. قُلْتُ وَاللَّهِ إِنِّي لَأُحِبُّ قُرْبَكَ وَأُحِبُّ مَا سَرَّكَ. قَالَتْ فَقَامَ فَتَطَهَّرَ ثُمَّ قَامَ يُصَلِّي فَلَمْ يَزَلْ يَبْكِي حَتَّى بَلَّ حِجْرَهُ ثُمَّ بَكَى فَلَمْ يَزَلْ يَبْكِي حَتَّى بَلَّ لِحْيَتَهُ ثُمَّ بَكَى فَلَمْ يَزَلْ يَبْكِي حَتَّى بَلَّ الْأَرْضَ فَجَاءَ بِلَالٌ يُؤْذِنُهُ بِالصَّلَاةِ فَلَمَّا رَآهُ يَبْكِي قَالَ يَا رَسُولَ اللَّهِ لِمَ تَبْكِي وَقَدْ غَفَرَ اللَّهُ لَكَ مَا تَقَدَّمَ وَمَا تَأَخَّرَ. قَالَ أَفَلَا أَكُونُ عَبْدًا شَكُورًا لَقَدْ نَزَلَتْ عَلَيَّ اللَّيْلَةَ آيَةٌ وَيْلٌ لِمَنْ قَرَأَهَا وَلَمْ يَتَفَكَّرْ فِيهَا:

(إِنَّ فِي خَلْقِ ٱلسَّمَٰوَٰتِ وَٱلْأَرْضِ وَٱخْتِلَٰفِ ٱلَّيْلِ وَٱلنَّهَارِ لَءَايَٰتٍ لِّأُو۟لِى ٱلْأَلْبَٰبِ (١٩٠)

'Ā'ishah narrated:

"Allah's Messenger said to me on one of my nights,[220] ''Ā'ishah, leave me to worship my Lord tonight.' I said, 'By Allah, I love to be close to you and I love what pleases you.' He stood up, performed *wuḍū*, and stood in prayer. He continued weeping until the area around his eyes became soaked. He continued weeping until his beard was soaked. His weeping continued until the ground itself was soaked with tears. Bilāl came and announced the call to prayer. When he saw the Prophet weeping, he said, 'O Allah's Messenger, why do you weep when Allah has forgiven you for what you have done and what you will do?' The Prophet said, 'Shall I not then be a grateful servant? An *āyah* has been revealed to me tonight and woe to the one who recites it without reflection:[221]
'Indeed, in the creation of the heavens and the earth and the

---

[220] This refers to one of the nights in which it was the turn of Umm al-Mu'minīn Sayyidah 'Ā'ishah to host the Prophet in her home, as each wife would host him one by one.
[221] *Ṣaḥīḥ Ibn Ḥibbān*, 620.

alternation of the day and night there are signs for people of reason.'"[222]

Reflection is encouraged throughout the Qur'an. We are asked not only to recite the Qur'an constantly but to also reflect upon its meanings. Allah is not asking us to take the Truth of the Qur'an on faith alone but to reflect upon its meanings and engage our intellect. The false religions of the world seek to limit the intellects of their followers and stop them from asking questions, asking them to instead blindly accept whatever mental polytheistic gymnastics are required to believe in two gods or three gods or pantheons.

Atheism asks its adherents to follow whatever the ever-changing and fallible science of the day says, abandoning logic and Truth in favour of a purely materialistic worldview. Islam does neither of these things. Islam tells you to engage your mind and think upon the Truth, to use logic and reasoning, and look deeply into each matter. There is no requirement for you to just believe that a matter is too complicated to explain, nor to do away with the concept of objective truth. Islam teaches you to reflect.

A Muslimah should reflect on all these things. Allah has told us to reflect on the Heavens and the Earth, and the night and the day, as signs of the Creator and the Truth of Islam. The Prophet ﷺ, chosen amongst all of creation to be the most beloved of Allah spent the night reflecting on this *āyah* until his face, his beard, his clothes, even the very ground itself, became wet with his tears. As the traveller of the Night Journey and the one upon whom this *āyah* had been revealed, he knew the truth of these words better than anyone, and it made him *weep.*

Each of us should spend some time reflecting on this verse and reading the *tafsīrs* of our pious predecessors upon it. Reflecting upon the Qur'an as you recite it will give you a deeper connection to the Book. Think deeply upon its meanings and read at least one reliable

---

[222] Qur'an, 3:190.

tafsīr with a good teacher. Ask questions and engage in the study of the Book of Allah. Do not stop there, but reflect upon yourself and your own existence, on why you are here, on what your purpose is and whether you are fulfilling that purpose. Take account of yourself and your deeds; self-reflect. Become mindful of the Hereafter and reflect upon the createdness of this universe and its complete dependence upon Allah to even remain consistent and existent. Sayyidunā ʿAwn ibn ʿAbdullāh ﷺ narrates:

قُلْتُ لِأُمِّ الدَّرْدَاءِ رضي الله عنها أَيُّ عِبَادَةِ أَبِي الدَّرْدَاءِ كَانَ أَكْثَرَ؟ قَالَتْ التَّفَكُّرُ وَالِاعْتِبَارُ.

"I said to Umm al-Dardā' ﷺ, 'What act of worship did Abū al-Dardā' do most?' Umm al-Dardā' said, 'Reflection and deep consideration.'"[223]

[223] Ibn al-Mubārak, *al-Zuhd wa al-Raqā'iq*, 286.

35
She Remembers Allah

عَنْ عَائِشَةَ قَالَتْ:

كَانَ النَّبِيُّ صَلَّى اللهُ عَلَيْهِ وَسَلَّمَ يَذْكُرُ اللهَ عَلَى كُلِّ أَحْيَانِهِ.

ʿĀ'ishah said:

"The Prophet ﷺ would remember Allah at all times."[224]

Reflecting upon Allah and remembering Allah are two different acts of worship, both of which are intrinsic aspects of Sufism and the internal spiritual path towards a Muslim's self-betterment. Reflection involves deep thought upon the Creator and His favours upon all of creation, starting with oneself and expanding to encompass the entirety of the universe. One could spend a lifetime reflecting upon Allah and not even glimpse the Truth of His Mercy, His Might, or His Wisdom.

Remembering Allah involves the deliberate action of being mindful of Him, praising Him, and glorifying Him. This is referred to as *dhikr*. Every time we say '*Subḥān Allāh*', '*Alḥamdulillāh*', '*Allāhu Akbar*', or '*Lā Ilāha il Allah*', we are engaged in this practice.

Some Muslims will read the term 'Sufism' and ascribe it to a particular sect or group, but this is a misapplication of the term. *Taṣawwuf* is the practice of spiritual purification through the worship and remembrance of Allah and has always been a part of Islam. It is the path of *iḥsān*. It derives its principles and practices from the actions of the pious predecessors, with many Sufi pathways tracing their chain of teachers back to Sayyidunā ʿAlī ﷺ, who himself learned from Allah's Messenger ﷺ. It should be understood that each of us engage in some form of this practice whenever we stand for *ṣalāh* or hold a set of prayer beads in our hands. The remembrance of Allah was a

---

[224] *Ṣaḥīḥ Muslim*, 373.

constant practice of the Prophet ﷺ, and there was never a time he was not engaged in *dhikr*.

One may wonder how to emulate such a practice. Is it possible for a regular Muslim to be *this* mindful of Allah, and constantly remember Him, and thus bring spirituality and worship into every moment of one's life, as the Prophet ﷺ did? Umm al-Mu'minīn Sayyidah ʿĀ'ishah ؓ narrates:

كَانَ النَّبِيُّ صَلَّى اللَّهُ عَلَيْهِ وَسَلَّمَ يُعْجِبُهُ التَّيَمُّنُ فِي تَنَعُّلِهِ وَتَرَجُّلِهِ وَطُهُورِهِ وَفِي شَأْنِهِ كُلِّهِ

"The Prophet ﷺ liked to begin from the right when putting on his shoes, combing his hair, performing his ablution, and in all of his affairs."[225]

Umm al-Mu'minīn Sayyidah ʿĀ'ishah ؓ also narrates:

كَانَ النَّبِيُّ صَلَّى اللَّهُ عَلَيْهِ وَسَلَّمَ يَأْكُلُ طَعَامًا فِي سِتَّةٍ مِنْ أَصْحَابِهِ فَجَاءَ أَعْرَابِيٌّ فَأَكَلَهُ بِلُقْمَتَيْنِ فَقَالَ رَسُولُ اللَّهِ صَلَّى اللَّهُ عَلَيْهِ وَسَلَّمَ أَمَا إِنَّهُ لَوْ سَمَّى لَكَفَاكُمْ

"The Prophet ﷺ was eating amongst six of his Ṣaḥābah when a Bedouin came and ate all of the food in two bites. The Prophet ﷺ said, 'If he had invoked the name of Allah, it would have sufficed you all.'"[226]

This is how we make every moment we live a mindful one and every act we do a form of worship. Each action we take should be deliberate, carried out in the best possible way with our minds focused on how we can please our Lord through the action, no matter how trivial it may be. By beginning all good tasks with the right, by invoking Allah's name when we begin anything worth beginning, and by following the Sunnah of the Prophet ﷺ in every aspect of our lives, we can ensure we are constantly in a state of remembrance and worship. Each of us must use the bathroom, but even carrying out this lowly yet necessary task can become beneficial to us if done with the Sunnah of Allah's Messenger

---

[225] *Ṣaḥīḥ al-Bukhārī*, 168; *Ṣaḥīḥ Muslim*, 268.
[226] *Jāmiʿ al-Tirmidhī*, 1858.

ﷺ in mind. We all have sexual desires, but if we fulfil them within the laws of the Sharia and in adherence to the Sunnah, then this too becomes a *ṣadaqah* and an act of worship. Islam is not difficult to follow once we begin to understand the universality of it. Every aspect of our lives can be shaped by the practice of the constant remembrance of Allah. Every deed can become an act of devout worship.

The people that do this, are acutely aware of Allah's favour upon us, and remember Him constantly, have a positive effect on us whenever they are near. Their mannerisms, the way they walk and talk, their piety, and their constant remembrance of Allah are such that we need not even be in their company, but only look upon them and we will find ourselves remembering Allah too. Sayyidah Asmā' bint Yazīd رضي الله عنها narrated:

قَالَ النَّبِيُّ صَلَّى اللَّهُ عَلَيْهِ وَسَلَّمَ أَلا أُخْبِرُكُمْ بِخِيَارِكُمْ؟ قَالُوا بَلَى! قَالَ الَّذِينَ إِذَا رُءُوا ذُكِرَ اللَّهُ. أَفَلا أُخْبِرُكُمْ بِشِرَارِكُمْ؟ قَالُوا بَلَى! قَالَ الْمَشَّاؤُونَ بِالنَّمِيمَةِ الْمُفْسِدُونَ بَيْنَ الأَحِبَّةِ الْبَاغُونَ الْبُرَآءَ الْعَنَتَ.

"The Prophet ﷺ said, 'Shall I not tell you about the best of you?' They[227] replied, 'Of course!' The Prophet ﷺ said, 'Those whose sight alone reminds you of Allah. Shall I not tell you about the worst of you?' They said, 'Of course.' The Prophet ﷺ said, 'Those who carry gossip, ruin relations between loved ones, and seek misery for the innocent.'"[228]

The polar opposite of a person who reminds you of Allah by their sight alone is the one who carries gossip and rumours, who breaks down family relationships, and wishes to harm people who have not harmed them. These actions describe Shayṭān, and yet they also describe the devils in human form that live amongst us, Muslim and non-Muslim alike. Shun such people and steer clear of them, lest you become like them through association. Bring spirituality and worship

[227] Meaning the Ṣaḥābah رضي الله عنهم.

[228] *Al-Adab al-Mufrad*, 323.

into every aspect of your life, and seek to remember Allah throughout your days and nights. This is the path to spiritual excellence and the path of the Prophet ﷺ.

36

She has *Taqwā*

عَنْ دُرَّةَ بِنْتِ أَبِي لَهَبٍ قَالَتْ:

قَامَ رَجُلٌ إِلَى النَّبِيِّ صَلَّى اللهُ عَلَيْهِ وَسَلَّمَ وَهُوَ عَلَى الْمِنْبَرِ فَقَالَ يَا رَسُولَ اللهِ أَيُّ النَّاسِ خَيْرٌ؟ فَقَالَ صَلَّى اللهُ عَلَيْهِ وَسَلَّمَ خَيْرُ النَّاسِ أَقْرَؤُهُمْ وَأَتْقَاهُمْ وَآمَرُهُمْ بِالْمَعْرُوفِ وَأَنْهَاهُمْ عَنِ الْمُنْكَرِ وَأَوْصَلُهُمْ لِلرَّحِمِ.

Durrah bint Abū Lahab narrated:

"A man stood before the Prophet ﷺ while he was upon the pulpit, and said, 'O Allah's Messenger, who are the best of people?' He replied, 'The best of people recite the most Qur'an, have the most *taqwā*, enjoin good the most and forbid evil the most, and maintain family ties the most.'"[229]

In the above hadith, the Prophet ﷺ listed five qualities of the best of people. That such people recite the Qur'an more than others should be clear - those who constantly recite the Qur'an are constantly connected to the highest knowledge and wisdom. The Divine Word of Allah is passing through their eyes, occupying their hearts and minds, and leaving their lips constantly. Enjoining good and forbidding evil were looked at in detail earlier in this book, as was the maintaining of family ties. The second quality listed, after constancy in the recitation of the Qur'an, is being the one with the most *taqwā*.

Taqwā is cognisance of Allah. It is the awareness that Allah is Ever Watchful and All-Seeing and the understanding that our actions will be means for our salvation or doom.

إِنَّ رَبَّكَ لَبِالْمِرْصَادِ (١٤)

"Your Lord is truly vigilant."[230]

---

[229] *Musnad al-Imām Aḥmad*, 27434.
[230] Qur'an, 89:14.

A person who is mindful of Allah at all times cannot sin or even approach sin. She does whatever she can to avoid it. If she mistakenly sins, she cannot rest until she has sought forgiveness for her transgression. She spends her time trying to please her Creator, for she knows that He is Watching her every action. She finds joy in what pleases Him. This is *taqwā*.

When one is unable to sin and is striving to find opportunities to please Allah, there can be no doubt as to the result of such piety and devotedness to Allah. Allah has listed the rewards for such people in the Qur'an. Allah says:

إِنَّ لِلْمُتَّقِينَ مَفَازًا (٣١)

"Indeed, the righteous will have salvation."[231]

Taqwā is not practised for any other reason but to please our Creator. However, two further benefits have been listed by Allah for the ones who internalise this mindset and become truly cognisant of Allah. The first of these is salvation. Each of us is sinful. It is unlikely that there is anyone alive today who has not sinned in some way at some point in their life. However, the people of *taqwā* have the advantage of being quick to rectify their mistakes and seek Allah's forgiveness. Through this quality they earn Allah's love, which brings them salvation and will *in shā Allāh* be a means of emancipation from the Fire. Regarding the second benefit, Allah says:

إِنَّ ٱلْمُتَّقِينَ فِى ظِلَـٰلٍ وَعُيُونٍ (٤١) وَفَوَٰكِهَ مِمَّا يَشْتَهُونَ (٤٢) كُلُوا۟ وَٱشْرَبُوا۟ هَنِيٓـًٔا بِمَا كُنتُمْ تَعْمَلُونَ (٤٣) إِنَّا كَذَٰلِكَ نَجْزِى ٱلْمُحْسِنِينَ (٤٤)

"Indeed, the righteous will be amid shade and springs and any fruit they desire. [They will be told:] 'Eat and drink happily for what you used to do.' Surely this is how We reward the good-doers."[232]

Paradise is their reward for seeking Allah's Pleasure and protection from His Wrath. The best women are thus those that have *taqwā*, for

---

[231] Qur'an, 78:31.
[232] Qur'an, 77:41-44.

they are the best of them in this world, the best of them on the Day of Requital, and the best of them ever after. Recall the hadith narrated by Sayyidunā Abū Udhaynah al-Ṣadafī ؓ from earlier:

خَيْرُ نِسَائِكُمُ الْوَدُودُ الْوَلُودُ الْمُوَاتِيَةُ الْمُوَاسِيَةُ إِذَا اتَّقَيْنَ اللَّهَ.

"The best of your women are loving, fertile, favourable, and comforting, when they are cognisant of Allah."[233]

These are the words of Allah's Messenger ﷺ. The best women are not only people of *taqwā* themselves, but they are blessings from Allah that assist their husbands in becoming better too, for the men in their lives also have the same goal. Sayyidunā Anas ibn Mālik ؓ narrates that Allah's Messenger ﷺ said,

مَنْ رَزَقَهُ اللَّهُ امْرَأَةً صَالِحَةً فَقَدْ أَعَانَهُ اللَّهُ عَلَى شَطْرِ دِينِهِ فَلْيَتَّقِ اللَّهَ فِي الشَّطْرِ الثَّانِي.

"Whoever Allah provides with a righteous wife, Allah has assisted him in half of his religion. Let him fear Allah regarding the second half."[234]

The level of one's *taqwā* correlates directly with one's position in the Sight of Allah. One's social status in this world or the eyes of the people has no effect on one's status before Allah. Rich or poor, free or slave, famous or forgotten, none of these things have a bearing on one's true status or virtue. Unlike other faiths or ideologies, Islam does not place any race or social class on a pedestal. Sayyidunā Abū Dharr ؓ narrated that Allah's Messenger ﷺ said,

انْظُرْ فَإِنَّكَ لَيْسَ بِخَيْرٍ مِنْ أَحْمَرَ وَلَا أَسْوَدَ إِلَّا أَنْ تَفْضُلَهُ بِتَقْوَى.

"Behold! Indeed you are neither better than the white one nor the black one, except in taqwā."[235]

Taqwā either makes or breaks a person's Hereafter. One's cultural heritage, skin colour, or country of birth does not dictate their true

---

[233] *Al-Sunan al-Kubrā*, 12480.
[234] *Al-Muʿjam al-Awsaṭ*, 992.
[235] *Musnad al-Imām Aḥmad*, 20885.

position in this life or the next, and it matters not if one is lowly in the eyes of the people. Islam removed tribalism as an idea. Sayyidah Umm al-Ḥusayn al-Aḥmasiyyah ؓ narrated:

سَمِعْتُ رَسُولَ اللَّهِ صلى الله عليه وسلم يَخْطُبُ فِي حَجَّةِ الْوَدَاعِ وَعَلَيْهِ بُرْدٌ قَدِ الْتَفَعَ بِهِ مِنْ تَحْتِ إِبْطِهِ قَالَتْ فَأَنَا أَنْظُرُ إِلَى عَضَلَةِ عَضُدِهِ تَرْتَجُّ سَمِعْتُهُ يَقُولُ يَا أَيُّهَا النَّاسُ اتَّقُوا اللَّهَ وَإِنْ أُمِّرَ عَلَيْكُمْ عَبْدٌ حَبَشِيٌّ مُجَدَّعٌ فَاسْمَعُوا لَهُ وَأَطِيعُوا مَا أَقَامَ لَكُمْ كِتَابَ اللَّهِ.

"I heard Allah's Messenger ﷺ delivering a sermon during the Farewell Hajj, and he was wearing a burd[236] which he had wrapped under his arm. I saw the muscles of his upper arm quivering as I heard him say: 'O people! Fear Allah! If a curly-haired Ḥabashī slave is given command over you, listen to him and obey him so long as he upholds the Book of Allah amongst you.'"[237]

Taqwā is the yardstick by which we are measured. Cognisance of Allah, an awareness of His Ever-Watchful nature, and protecting oneself from ever nearing disobedience to Him – these are the qualities that grant superiority of one human being over another. Colour, race, culture, or geographical origin have no bearing on one's success or failure in the Sight of Allah, and thus Islam disregards such things.

Guard yourself from ever approaching sin. Be cognisant of Allah and create a barrier of safety between your righteous self and the outside world, lest it taint you by association. The barrier is *taqwā* and it is formed spiritually through building an awareness of the All-Seeing, and physically through obedience to the commands of hijab. Allah says:

يَٰبَنِىٓ ءَادَمَ قَدْ أَنزَلْنَا عَلَيْكُمْ لِبَاسًا يُوَٰرِى سَوْءَٰتِكُمْ وَرِيشًا ۖ وَلِبَاسُ ٱلتَّقْوَىٰ ذَٰلِكَ خَيْرٌ ۚ ذَٰلِكَ مِنْ ءَايَٰتِ ٱللَّهِ لَعَلَّهُمْ يَذَّكَّرُونَ.

---

[236] A style of cloak.
[237] *Jāmiʿ al-Tirmidhī*, 1706.

"O children of Adam! We have provided for you clothing to cover your nakedness and as an adornment. However, the best clothing is righteousness. This is one of Allah's bounties, so perhaps you will be mindful."[238]

[238] Qur'an, 7:26.

37
She Practises *Tawakkul*

عَنْ أَبِي سَعِيدٍ:

جَاءَتْ امْرَأَةٌ إِلَى رَسُولِ اللهِ صَلَّى اللهُ عَلَيْهِ وَسَلَّمَ فَقَالَتْ يَا رَسُولَ اللهِ ذَهَبَ الرِّجَالُ بِحَدِيثِكَ فَاجْعَلْ لَنَا مِنْ نَفْسِكَ يَوْمًا نَأْتِيكَ فِيهِ تُعَلِّمُنَا مِمَّا عَلَّمَكَ اللهُ. فَقَالَ اجْتَمِعْنَ فِي يَوْمِ كَذَا وَكَذَا فِي مَكَانِ كَذَا وَكَذَا. فَاجْتَمَعْنَ فَأَتَاهُنَّ رَسُولُ اللهِ صَلَّى اللهُ عَلَيْهِ وَسَلَّمَ فَعَلَّمَهُنَّ مِمَّا عَلَّمَهُ اللهُ ثُمَّ قَالَ: مَا مِنْكُنَّ امْرَأَةٌ تُقَدِّمُ بَيْنَ يَدَيْهَا مِنْ وَلَدِهَا ثَلَاثَةً إِلَّا كَانَ لَهَا حِجَابًا مِنْ النَّارِ. فَقَالَتْ امْرَأَةٌ مِنْهُنَّ يَا رَسُولَ اللهِ أَوْ اثْنَيْنِ؟ قَالَ فَأَعَادَتْهَا مَرَّتَيْنِ. ثُمَّ قَالَ وَاثْنَيْنِ وَاثْنَيْنِ وَاثْنَيْنِ.

Abū Saʿīd al-Khudrī narrated:

"A woman came to Allah's Messenger ﷺ and said, 'O Allah's Messenger, the men benefit from your speeches. Please set a day for us when we can come to you and you can teach us what Allah has taught you.' The Prophet ﷺ said, 'Gather on such-and-such a day at such-and-such a place.' And so they gathered and the Prophet ﷺ came and taught them what Allah had taught him. He then said, 'No woman among you will lose three children except that they will shield her from the Hellfire.' A woman asked, 'O Allah's Messenger, what of two children?' She repeated her question twice more and the Prophet ﷺ said, 'Even two, even two, even two.'"[239]

Tawakkul is the practice of giving oneself entirely to the Will of Allah. It is complete acceptance of the idea that Allah controls all things in the universe and that nothing can occur without His Divine Will. Everything happens in accordance with His Perfect Plan. As humans, we cannot comprehend this plan, nor even observe a single branch of its myriad intricacies. We therefore fall foul of our own lack of intellect, lamenting the 'affliction' of fate upon us instead of realising the fundamental truth that Allah is the All-Merciful and the Very-Merciful,

[239] *Ṣaḥīḥ al-Bukhārī*, 7310; *Ṣaḥīḥ Muslim*, 2634.

and His plan has taken into account all the perceived harm that one may suffer in life.

Even when we go through extreme distress, this too is from the Will of Allah. To Him we belong and to Him we return. Allah says:

يَـٰٓأَيُّهَا ٱلَّذِينَ ءَامَنُوا۟ ٱسْتَعِينُوا۟ بِٱلصَّبْرِ وَٱلصَّلَوٰةِ ۚ إِنَّ ٱللَّهَ مَعَ ٱلصَّـٰبِرِينَ (١٥٣) وَلَا تَقُولُوا۟
لِمَن يُقْتَلُ فِى سَبِيلِ ٱللَّهِ أَمْوَٰتٌۢ ۚ بَلْ أَحْيَآءٌ وَلَـٰكِن لَّا تَشْعُرُونَ (١٥٤) وَلَنَبْلُوَنَّكُم بِشَىْءٍ مِّنَ
ٱلْخَوْفِ وَٱلْجُوعِ وَنَقْصٍ مِّنَ ٱلْأَمْوَٰلِ وَٱلْأَنفُسِ وَٱلثَّمَرَٰتِ ۗ وَبَشِّرِ ٱلصَّـٰبِرِينَ (١٥٥) ٱلَّذِينَ إِذَآ
أَصَـٰبَتْهُم مُّصِيبَةٌ قَالُوٓا۟ إِنَّا لِلَّهِ وَإِنَّآ إِلَيْهِ رَٰجِعُونَ (١٥٦) أُو۟لَـٰٓئِكَ عَلَيْهِمْ صَلَوَٰتٌ مِّن رَّبِّهِمْ
وَرَحْمَةٌ ۖ وَأُو۟لَـٰٓئِكَ هُمُ ٱلْمُهْتَدُونَ (١٥٧)

"O believers! Seek comfort in patience and prayer. Allah is truly with those who are patient. Never say that those martyred in the cause of Allah are dead - in fact, they are alive! But you do not perceive it. We will certainly test you with a touch of fear and famine and loss of property, life, and crops. Give good news to those who patiently endure - who say, when struck by a disaster, 'Surely to Allah we belong and to Him we will return.' They are the ones who will receive Allah's blessings and mercy. And it is they who are guided."[240]

Any and all afflictions are from Allah; they are tests through which we can gain ultimate success if we bear them with patience. It is easy to praise Allah when He bestows blessings upon you in this world, but it is far more difficult to do so when calamity strikes. When a child is born, we say "All praise is for Allah!" But what about when a child dies? Allah has given glad tidings to those who suffer calamity and face it with patience and perseverance and has promised in the Qur'an to grant such stalwarts of faith His Divine Blessings and Mercy. *Tawakkul* involves having a complete reliance on Allah; that is, not just the reliance that we as the creation must have on the Creator to even exist, for all things rely on Allah in this way, but to rely on Allah in all our affairs. *Tawakkul* means to turn to Him and ask for His help in every situation and to know and understand that He has decreed that

[240] Qur'an, 2:153-157.

whatever you are going through is a test from Him and that relief from whatever burden you are given will only be granted through Him.

لَا يُكَلِّفُ ٱللَّهُ نَفْسًا إِلَّا وُسْعَهَا ۚ لَهَا مَا كَسَبَتْ وَعَلَيْهَا مَا ٱكْتَسَبَتْ ۗ رَبَّنَا لَا تُؤَاخِذْنَآ إِن نَّسِينَآ أَوْ أَخْطَأْنَا ۚ رَبَّنَا وَلَا تَحْمِلْ عَلَيْنَآ إِصْرًا كَمَا حَمَلْتَهُۥ عَلَى ٱلَّذِينَ مِن قَبْلِنَا ۚ رَبَّنَا وَلَا تُحَمِّلْنَا مَا لَا طَاقَةَ لَنَا بِهِۦ ۖ وَٱعْفُ عَنَّا وَٱغْفِرْ لَنَا وَٱرْحَمْنَآ ۚ أَنتَ مَوْلَىٰنَا فَٱنصُرْنَا عَلَى ٱلْقَوْمِ ٱلْكَٰفِرِينَ (٢٨٦)

"Allah does not require of any soul more than what it can afford. All good will be for its own benefit, and all evil will be to its own loss. [The believers pray:] 'Our Lord! Do not punish us if we forget or make a mistake. Our Lord! Do not place a burden on us like the one You placed on those before us. Our Lord! Do not burden us with what we cannot bear. Pardon us, forgive us, and have mercy on us. You are our Guardian. So grant us victory over the disbelieving people.'"[241]

This is the route to inner peace, regardless of the situation we are put in. Whether it is the death of several of our children, or only the slightest prick from a thorn, each of us should hold fast to the path of *tawakkul.* Sayyidunā Jābir ﵁ narrated that Allah's Messenger ﷺ said,

مَا مِنْ مُؤْمِنٍ وَلَا مُؤْمِنَةٍ وَلَا مُسْلِمٍ وَلَا مَسْلَمَةٍ يَمْرَضُ مَرَضًا إِلَّا قَصَّ اللَّهُ بِهِ عَنْهُ مِنْ خَطَايَاهُ

"No believing man or woman, nor Muslim man or woman, is afflicted with illness except that Allah will curtail their sins."[242]

Sayyidah Umm 'Umārah bint Ka'b al-Anṣārī ﵂ narrated,

أَنَّ النَّبِيَّ صَلَّى اللَّهُ عَلَيْهِ وَسَلَّمَ دَخَلَ عَلَيْهَا فَقَدَّمَتْ إِلَيْهِ طَعَامًا فَقَالَ كُلِي. فَقَالَتْ إِنِّي صَائِمَةٌ. فَقَالَ رَسُولُ اللَّهِ صَلَّى اللَّهُ عَلَيْهِ وَسَلَّمَ إِنَّ الصَّائِمَ تُصَلِّي عَلَيْهِ الْمَلَائِكَةُ إِذَا أُكِلَ عِنْدَهُ حَتَّى يَفْرُغُوا.

The Prophet ﷺ entered her home and she served him food. He asked, "Will you eat?" She said, "I am fasting." Allah's Messenger

---

241 Qur'an, 2:286.
242 *Al-Adab al-Mufrad*, 508.

said, *"Indeed the angels send blessings upon a fasting person when others eat in their presence until they finish."*[243]

How, then, should we react when we face hardships, great or small? As stated above, one way is to state '*alḥamdulillāh*' and another is to state '*innā lillāhi wa innā ilayhi rājiʿūn*'. Sayyidah Asmā' bint ʿUmays ؓ narrated that Allah's Messenger ﷺ advised,

مَنْ أَصَابَهُ هَمٌّ أَوْ غَمٌّ أَوْ سَقَمٌ أَوْ شِدَّةٌ فَقَالَ "اللهُ رَبِّي لَا شَرِيكَ لَهُ" كَشَفَ ذَلِكَ عَنْهُ.

"Whoever is afflicted by anxiety, grief, illness, or hardship and says, 'Allah is my Lord, He has no partner', it will be lifted off him."[244]

Life is a struggle. It is designed to test us. No one will ever go through life without facing some form of hardship or test, and thus it would be foolish of us not to prepare ourselves beforehand, to steel ourselves against whatever may come. Sayyidah Umm al-Dardā' ؓ narrated that Sayyidunā Abū al-Dardā' ؓ said,

مَنْ قَالَ إِذَا أَصْبَحَ وَإِذَا أَمْسَى 'حَسْبِيَ اللَّهُ لَا إِلَهَ إِلَّا هُوَ عَلَيْهِ تَوَكَّلْتُ وَهُوَ رَبُّ الْعَرْشِ الْعَظِيمِ' سَبْعَ مَرَّاتٍ كَفَاهُ اللَّهُ مَا أَهَمَّهُ صَادِقًا كَانَ بِهَا أَوْ كَاذِبًا .

"Whoever repeats, 'Allah suffices me; there is no god but He. I trust in Him, and He is the Lord of the Supreme Throne,' seven times in the morning and evening, Allah will suffice him against anything that grieves him, whether he is true or false in (repeating) them."[245]

Having complete *tawakkul* will lead to one becoming more and more inclined towards asceticism[246] as they come to realise that this life is only a test and that any form of indulgence is merely a distraction from this truth. This is not something to shy away from, but a goal we should have. When we realise this Truth, all our anxieties and grief will slip away and we will be left with a deep inner peace. Sayyidunā Abū

---

[243] *Jāmiʿ al-Tirmidhī*, 785.
[244] *Al-Muʿjam al-Kabīr*, vol. 24, p. 154.
[245] *Sunan Abī Dāwūd*, 5081.
[246] Self-discipline and an aversion to indulgence.

al-Dardā' ﷺ was known, even amongst the Ṣaḥābah ﷺ, for this quality.

In the end, all of this is easier said than done, and many of us will struggle and stumble when hardship comes our way. It is our sincerest prayer that you are never tested with any great afflictions, but if Allah decrees that you are to be tested then turn only to Him for aid and take solace in His Word. As the Messengers ﷺ said to the disbelievers:

وَمَا لَنَآ أَلَّا نَتَوَكَّلَ عَلَى ٱللَّهِ وَقَدْ هَدَىٰنَا سُبُلَنَا ۚ وَلَنَصْبِرَنَّ عَلَىٰ مَآ ءَاذَيْتُمُونَا ۚ وَعَلَى ٱللَّهِ فَلْيَتَوَكَّلِ ٱلْمُتَوَكِّلُونَ.

"What is wrong with us that we should not put our trust in Allah when He has guided us to our paths? We shall, of course, endure with patience all your persecutions; and all those who have to trust should trust only in Allah."[247]

[247] Qur'an, 14:12.

38
She is Grateful

عَنْ عَائِشَةَ ـ رضى الله عنها ـ أَنَّ نَبِيَّ اللَّهِ صلى الله عليه وسلم كَانَ يَقُومُ مِنَ اللَّيْلِ حَتَّى تَتَفَطَّرَ قَدَمَاهُ فَقَالَتْ عَائِشَةُ لِمَ تَصْنَعُ هَذَا يَا رَسُولَ اللَّهِ وَقَدْ غَفَرَ اللَّهُ لَكَ مَا تَقَدَّمَ مِنْ ذَنْبِكَ وَمَا تَأَخَّرَ؟ قَالَ أَفَلاَ أُحِبُّ أَنْ أَكُونَ عَبْدًا شَكُورًا؟ فَلَمَّا كَثُرَ لَحْمُهُ صَلَّى جَالِسًا فَإِذَا أَرَادَ أَنْ يَرْكَعَ قَامَ، فَقَرَأَ ثُمَّ رَكَعَ.

ʿĀ'ishah ﵂ narrated:

"The Prophet ﷺ would stand in prayer at night until his feet would swell. I said, 'Why do you do this, O Allah's Messenger, when Allah has forgiven you your mistakes of the past and those to come?' He said, 'Should I not then love to be a thankful slave?' When he grew old, he would pray sitting, yet when he intended to bow he would stand, recite further, and then bow."[248]

Gratitude and thankfulness to Allah are a necessity. He is our Creator, our Sustainer, and our Nourisher. When we are sinful, He is All-Forgiving; when we are harmed, He is the Just. When we cry out in weakness, the All-Hearing and All-Powerful Hears our wails; when we call for help, He alone is our Helper. The Qur'an's opening four verses encapsulate this relationship:

ٱلْحَمْدُ لِلَّهِ رَبِّ ٱلْعَـٰلَمِينَ (١) ٱلرَّحْمَـٰنِ ٱلرَّحِيمِ (٢) مَـٰلِكِ يَوْمِ ٱلدِّينِ (٣) إِيَّاكَ نَعْبُدُ وَإِيَّاكَ نَسْتَعِينُ (٤)

"All praise is for Allah - Lord of all worlds, the Most Compassionate, Most Merciful, Master of the Day of Judgment. You we worship and You we ask for help."[249]

The Prophet ﷺ would spend his nights in prayers, so much so that his feet would swell from the strain of standing so long in prayer. He had been forgiven all of his mistakes, past and future, and thus he could

---

[248] *Ṣaḥīḥ al-Bukhārī*, 4837.
[249] Qur'an, 1:1-4.

not do anything but praise Allah throughout the night, in unreserved gratitude for the favours He had bestowed upon him.

Many of us struggle in life, we suffer many hardships and strive through many trials. In such states it is easy for us, as the weak slaves of Allah, to forget what Allah has granted us. A Muslimah should be ever thankful to Allah for what she has been given. Every moment we are alive is a blessing. At any point, Allah could remove from us the laws of physics, or the fundamental order of the universe and we would cease to exist. It is Allah's eternal favour on mankind that such things continue to work with perfect precision. Imagine if water or oxygen were scarce and we had to fight for every sip or breath. It is a great blessing that Allah has granted us whatever we need in abundance.

Allah has granted us our lives and every breath is a blessing, every thought a boon. Ask the woman who has lost her sight what a blessing your eyesight is and she will tell you. Ask the amputee what she would give to hold her husband's hand once more and her tears will answer. You are, by your very existence, blessed.

Allah has chosen you above all creation to be a human being. He has given you the ability to be a believer. Many of you were no doubt born believers, and born into believing families. Ask the reverts how they struggled to find the truth and accept it, and what trials they faced from their families and friends when they finally did. Further still, Allah has made you a Muslim from the greatest Ummah, the Ummah of the Final Prophet ﷺ. If we were to attempt to enumerate the blessings that Allah has given us, we would run out of ink and paper before the list came close to completion. A lifetime is not long enough to list His blessings upon us. How, then, can we not be grateful to Him?

فَبِأَيِّ ءَالَآءِ رَبِّكُمَا تُكَذِّبَانِ (١٣)

"Then which of your Lord's favours will you both deny?"[250]

[250] Qur'an, 55:13.

So, a Muslimah is grateful, but further to this she also has an aversion to ungratefulness. Too often we find ourselves lost to our own whims and wishes, and this results in becoming unthankful for what we have as we long for what we have not. Ask yourself: when your husband brings home groceries, but he has missed some ingredients that you asked for, do you thank him for what he brought or berate him for the missing ingredients? When your mother makes you food, are you grateful that there is food on the table or do you complain that she has not made you a particular dish?

Sayyidunā Ibn ʿAbbās narrated:

قَالَ النَّبِيُّ صلى الله عليه وسلم أُرِيتُ النَّارَ فَإِذَا أَكْثَرُ أَهْلِهَا النِّسَاءُ يَكْفُرْنَ. قِيلَ أَيَكْفُرْنَ بِاللَّهِ؟ قَالَ يَكْفُرْنَ الْعَشِيرَ، وَيَكْفُرْنَ الْإِحْسَانَ، لَوْ أَحْسَنْتَ إِلَى إِحْدَاهُنَّ الدَّهْرَ ثُمَّ رَأَتْ مِنْكَ شَيْئًا قَالَتْ مَا رَأَيْتُ مِنْكَ خَيْرًا قَطُّ.

"The Prophet said, 'I was shown the Fire; the majority of its dwellers were ungrateful women.' It was asked, 'Are they ungrateful to Allah?' He replied, 'They are ungrateful to their husbands and ungrateful for the good done to them. If you have always been good to one of them and then she sees something (not to her liking) in you, she will say, 'I have never received any good from you.'"[251]

The word *kufr* or 'disbelief' literally means 'ungratefulness'. The word is used in this hadith in its literal form, which was clarified when the people asked if the *kufr* was against Allah. Ungratefulness is a terrible disease, the results of which can be seen in the above hadith. How many of us are guilty of the example that the Prophet gave? It is worth reflecting on. No doubt every reader has either experienced this, or said something similar.

We are all guilty of these acts of ungratefulness, both to Allah and to our loved ones, but this forgetfulness is part of being human. What matters is that we recognise these faults and try to correct them, and work towards becoming *better*. Better mothers, daughters, sisters, and

---

[251] *Ṣaḥīḥ al-Bukhārī*, 29.

wives; better Muslimahs and better human beings. Being grateful for what we have and where we are in life is the first step to becoming this better version of yourself.

39
She Repents

عَنْ صَفِيَّةَ عَنْ عَائِشَةَ رضي الله عنها قَالَتْ:

طُوبَى لِمَنْ وَجَدَ فِي صَحِيفَتِهِ اسْتِغْفَارًا كَثِيرًا.

Ṣafiyyah reported that ʿĀ'ishah ﵂ said:

"Blessed is the one who finds abundant prayers for forgiveness on their record."[252]

All people carry two flaws: we are forgetful and we err. Forgetfulness is part of being human and is often the cause of the mistakes we make in life. Sometimes our desires carry us away and we forget that Allah is watching us. Sometimes we forget our previous mistakes and we make the same mistake again. Sayyidunā Anas ﵁ narrated that Allah's Messenger ﷺ said,

كُلُّ بَنِي آدَمَ خَطَّاءٌ وَخَيْرُ الْخَطَّائِينَ التَّوَّابُونَ.

"All the children of Adam make mistakes, and the best of those who make mistakes are those who repent."[253]

It is in our nature to falter and forget, but when we come to our senses, we must always seek Allah's forgiveness. As Umm al-Mu'minīn Sayyidah ʿĀ'ishah ﵂ stated, the ones who sought forgiveness the most will be the ones most blessed. We are all in need of Allah's Divine Mercy and Forgiveness; indeed, we are reliant on His favour to gain entry to Paradise. We sin so abundantly, and worship so poorly, that there is no other way to redemption except through His Divine Mercy.

The Prophet ﷺ himself would continuously seek Allah's forgiveness throughout the day, as Sayyidunā ʿAbdullāh ibn ʿUmar ﵄ narrated:

---

[252] *Shuʿab al-Īmān*, 646.

[253] *Sunan Ibn Mājah*, 4251.

كَانَ يُعَدُّ لِرَسُولِ اللَّهِ صَلَّى اللَّهُ عَلَيْهِ وَسَلَّمَ فِي الْمَجْلِسِ الْوَاحِدِ مِائَةَ مَرَّةٍ مِنْ قَبْلِ أَنْ يَقُومَ: رَبِّ اغْفِرْ لِي وَتُبْ عَلَيَّ إِنَّكَ أَنْتَ التَّوَّابُ الْغَفُورُ.

"We counted Allah's Messenger ﷺ say the following one hundred times in a single sitting before standing: 'My Lord, forgive me and accept my repentance. Indeed, You Alone are the Relenting, the Forgiving.'"[254]

In fact, it was his practice to spend both day and night in seeking the forgiveness and mercy of Allah. It is this combination of the cognisance of Allah's watching you, wilfully and sincerely carrying out actions that please Him, and repenting for the mistakes we make and sins we commit which will ultimately lead to our salvation. Umm al-Mu'minīn Sayyidah 'Ā'ishah ؓ narrated:

فَقَدْتُ رَسُولَ اللَّهِ ـ صلى الله عليه وسلم ـ ذَاتَ لَيْلَةٍ مِنْ فِرَاشِهِ فَالْتَمَسْتُهُ فَوَقَعَتْ يَدِي عَلَى بَطْنِ قَدَمَيْهِ وَهُوَ فِي الْمَسْجِدِ وَهُمَا مَنْصُوبَتَانِ وَهُوَ يَقُولُ: اللَّهُمَّ إِنِّي أَعُوذُ بِرِضَاكَ مِنْ سَخَطِكَ وَبِمُعَافَاتِكَ مِنْ عُقُوبَتِكَ وَأَعُوذُ بِكَ مِنْكَ لاَ أُحْصِي ثَنَاءً عَلَيْكَ أَنْتَ كَمَا أَثْنَيْتَ عَلَى نَفْسِكَ.

"One night, I noticed that Allah's Messenger ﷺ was missing from his bedding, so I searched for him and my hand touched the soles of his feet. He was in the masjid with his feet upright,[255] saying: 'O Allah, I seek refuge in Your Pleasure from Your Wrath and in Your Forgiveness from Your Punishment. I seek refuge in You from You. I cannot praise You enough; You are as You have praised Yourself.'"[256]

This is the perfect example of our beloved Prophet ﷺ, his devotion to Allah, and his constancy in repentance and seeking forgiveness. In the dark of night, when even his wife was unaware of what he was doing, he was seeking Allah's mercy and refuge whilst prostrating in complete humility.

---

[254] *Jāmiʿ al-Tirmidhī*, 3434.
[255] Meaning the Prophet ﷺ was prostrating.
[256] *Sunan Ibn Mājah*, 3841.

Women have an advantage here, as they pray at home and therefore can conceal themselves from the eyes of others and ensure complete sincerity in their worship and their repentance.

The advice of the Prophet ﷺ to his wife regarding the Night of Power was no different. Umm al-Mu'minīn Sayyidah 'Ā'ishah ؓ narrated:

أَنَّهَا قَالَتْ يَا رَسُولَ اللَّهِ أَرَأَيْتَ إِنْ وَافَقْتُ لَيْلَةَ الْقَدْرِ مَا أَدْعُو؟ قَالَ تَقُولِينَ اللَّهُمَّ إِنَّكَ عَفُوٌّ تُحِبُّ الْعَفْوَ فَاعْفُ عَنِّي.

"I said, 'O Allah's Messenger, what should I say in my supplication, if I come upon the Night of Power?' He said, 'Say: O Allah, You are indeed forgiving and You love forgiveness, so forgive me.'"[257]

Many of us sin and do not even realise we are sinning, many of us sin so often the transgressions begin to appear quite small in the grand scheme of things. This is a trap from the traps of Shayṭān. He lulls us into inaction and sloth and then, like the venomous serpent he is, he bites us as we sleep. We must wake ourselves up from our spiritual slumber and correct our course before it is too late. Learn about your religion, understand the fundamentals of right and wrong, and hold yourself to account before you are held to account. Seek Allah's forgiveness constantly, both for the sins you are aware of and those you have become numb to. Salvation comes only through the Grace of Allah and the practices of His Prophet ﷺ, and as we have seen his practice was to spend day and night in abundant repentance.

Each of us are on our own journey, ever moving towards our own graves. We will spend much longer there than we spent outside of it, and the life of the Hereafter is forever. The world is a prison from which we will one day be released. Committing crimes in the world will lead to a far worse incarceration, whilst doing good will lead to a better life of infinite freedom in the Hereafter. Repent and correct yourself,

---

[257] *Sunan Ibn Mājah,* 3850.

not just by seeking forgiveness, but in the promise that you will no longer sin again. As people, we will slip and stumble as we race towards our goal in the Hereafter. The expectation is not for you to become sinless, but to strive to be so, to repent each time we fall into that same mistake, and to reaffirm our oath to not commit the sin again.

We are neither Angels, nor Prophets, nor those chosen to be amongst them, but neither are we animals or demons. We are human, we are Muslim, and we have a choice with regard to which of those listed we wish to be among. Choose the right target, and do your best to reach it.

40
She is Prepared for Death

عَنْ عَائِشَةَ قَالَتْ:

قَالَ رَسُولُ اللَّهِ صَلَّى اللَّهُ عَلَيْهِ وَسَلَّمَ مَنْ أَحَبَّ لِقَاءَ اللَّهِ أَحَبَّ اللَّهُ لِقَاءَهُ وَمَنْ كَرِهَ لِقَاءَ اللَّهِ كَرِهَ اللَّهُ لِقَاءَهُ. فَقُلْتُ يَا نَبِيَّ اللَّهِ أَكَرَاهِيَةُ الْمَوْتِ فَكُلُّنَا نَكْرَهُ الْمَوْتَ. فَقَالَ لَيْسَ كَذَلِكِ وَلَكِنَّ الْمُؤْمِنَ إِذَا بُشِّرَ بِرَحْمَةِ اللَّهِ وَرِضْوَانِهِ وَجَنَّتِهِ أَحَبَّ لِقَاءَ اللَّهِ فَأَحَبَّ اللَّهُ لِقَاءَهُ وَإِنَّ الْكَافِرَ إِذَا بُشِّرَ بِعَذَابِ اللَّهِ وَسَخَطِهِ كَرِهَ لِقَاءَ اللَّهِ وَكَرِهَ اللَّهُ لِقَاءَهُ

ʿĀ'ishah narrated:

"Allah's Messenger ﷺ said, 'Whoever loves to meet Allah, Allah loves to meet him; whoever hates to meet Allah, Allah hates to meet him.' I said, 'O Prophet of Allah, we all hate death and are averse to it.' He said, 'It is not like this. Rather, when a believer is given glad tidings of the Mercy of Allah, His Pleasure, and His Paradise, he loves to meet Allah and Allah loves to meet him. When a disbeliever receives the news of punishment from Allah and the hardship to be imposed by Him, he hates to meet Allah and Allah hates to meet him.'"[258]

The one guarantee we have in life is that death comes to us all. The princess and the prostitute, the teacher and the taught, the fair-minded and the foolish; none are spared. Prophets ﷺ have come to the world and have been taken from us; great tyrants have exerted their wills upon the people and have been swept away as a strong wind sweeps away footprints in the desert sands. Time is the great tide that erases all that stands before it, bringing death and leaving only memories and the deeds we wrought. As the tides of time continue to ebb and flow, even the memories of us will erode away.

Prepare for death, the inevitable adversary that cannot be defeated. The many qualities and attributes that have been listed in the preceding pages are for naught if we fail at the last hurdle. We should not fear

---

[258] *Ṣaḥīḥ Muslim*, 157.

death any more than we fear the cycle of day and night, for life and death is merely another binary cycle that Allah has set in motion in the universe. All created things begin and all of them end. Even death will end one day. Allah Alone is Eternal.

Sayyidunā Abū Hurayrah ﵁ narrated that Allah's Messenger ﷺ said,

يُؤْتَى بِالْمَوْتِ يَوْمَ الْقِيَامَةِ فَيُوقَفُ عَلَى الصِّرَاطِ فَيُقَالُ يَا أَهْلَ الْجَنَّةِ . فَيَطَّلِعُونَ خَائِفِينَ وَجِلِينَ أَنْ يُخْرَجُوا مِنْ مَكَانِهِمُ الَّذِي هُمْ فِيهِ. ثُمَّ يُقَالُ يَا أَهْلَ النَّارِ فَيَطَّلِعُونَ مُسْتَبْشِرِينَ فَرِحِينَ أَنْ يُخْرَجُوا مِنْ مَكَانِهِمُ الَّذِي هُمْ فِيهِ. فَيُقَالُ هَلْ تَعْرِفُونَ هَذَا؟ قَالُوا نَعَمْ هَذَا الْمَوْتُ. قَالَ فَيُؤْمَرُ بِهِ فَيُذْبَحُ عَلَى الصِّرَاطِ ثُمَّ يُقَالُ لِلْفَرِيقَيْنِ كِلاَهُمَا خُلُودٌ فِيمَا تَجِدُونَ لاَ مَوْتَ فِيهِ أَبَدًا .

"Death will be brought on the Day of Resurrection and made to stand on the Ṣirāṭ. It will be said, 'O people of Paradise!' And they will look up, anxious and afraid, lest they be brought out of the place they reside in. Then it will be said, 'O people of Hell!' And they will look up, hoping that they will be removed from the place they reside in. Then it will be said, 'Do you know what this is?' They will say, 'Yes, it is Death.' Then the Command will be given for it to be slaughtered on the Ṣirāṭ, and it will be said to both groups, 'Your residence is eternal, and there will never again be Death within it.'"[259]

Death is not the monster chasing you through life, as many a poet has tricked you into believing; death is the finish line. That is not to say that a Muslimah should throw her life away or race toward death, but that *when death comes* it is to be welcomed as glad tidings for the believer. Once that final hurdle is overcome, the tests of this world will be over and a believer can at last gladly accept the rewards that Allah promised her. As Allah says:

كُلُّ نَفْسٍ ذَآئِقَةُ ٱلْمَوْتِ ۖ ثُمَّ إِلَيْنَا تُرْجَعُونَ (٥٧)

"Every soul will taste death, then to Us you will be returned."[260]

---

[259] *Sunan Ibn Mājah*, 4327.
[260] Qur'an, 29:57.

Is returning to Allah not a thing to be desired? Umm al-Mu'minīn Sayyidah ʿĀ'ishah ﵂ narrated:

كَانَ النَّبِيُّ صلى الله عليه وسلم يَقُولُ وَهْوَ صَحِيحٌ: إِنَّهُ لَمْ يُقْبَضْ نَبِيٌّ حَتَّى يَرَى مَقْعَدَهُ مِنَ الْجَنَّةِ، ثُمَّ يُخَيَّرَ. فَلَمَّا نَزَلَ بِهِ وَرَأْسُهُ عَلَى فَخِذِي غُشِيَ عَلَيْهِ، ثُمَّ أَفَاقَ، فَأَشْخَصَ بَصَرَهُ إِلَى سَقْفِ الْبَيْتِ ثُمَّ قَالَ " اللَّهُمَّ الرَّفِيقَ الأَعْلَى ". فَقُلْتُ إِذًا لاَ يَخْتَارُنَا. وَعَرَفْتُ أَنَّهُ الْحَدِيثُ الَّذِي كَانَ يُحَدِّثُنَا وَهْوَ صَحِيحٌ قَالَتْ فَكَانَتْ آخِرَ كَلِمَةٍ تَكَلَّمَ بِهَا " اللَّهُمَّ الرَّفِيقَ الأَعْلَى ".

"When the Prophet ﷺ was healthy, he used to say, and it is true, 'No soul of a Prophet is taken until he is shown his place in Paradise and then he is given the option.' When death approached him whilst his head was on my lap, he became unconscious and then recovered his consciousness. He then looked at the ceiling of the house and said, 'O Allah, with the Highest Companion!' I said to myself, 'He is not going to choose us,' and I realised that this is what he had said to us when he was healthy. The last words he spoke were, 'O Allah, with the Highest Companion!'"[261]

The Prophet ﷺ was offered the companionship of Allah or the chance to live on. Having seen the truth of such a blessed opportunity, and having been shown it once more, his choice was clear and he was prepared.

The thought of death's inevitability should be a constant thought in the mind of every believer. If this is not doable, at the very least we should take time out of every day to take account of ourselves and our deeds, and to seek our betterment by begging Allah's forgiveness for our misdeeds and striving to be better in the time we have left. Every second from this very moment onward is one less second you have to secure your Hereafter. Sayyidunā Abū Yaʿlā Shaddād ibn Aws ﵁ narrated that Allah's Messenger ﷺ said,

الْكَيِّسُ مَنْ دَانَ نَفْسَهُ وَعَمِلَ لِمَا بَعْدَ الْمَوْتِ وَالْعَاجِزُ مَنْ أَتْبَعَ نَفْسَهُ هَوَاهَا ثُمَّ تَمَنَّى عَلَى اللَّهِ.

[261] *Ṣaḥīḥ al-Bukhārī*, 4463.

"The wise one takes account of himself and strives for what follows after death; the helpless one follows his whims and then engages in wishful thinking about Allah."[262]

The Mercy of Allah is infinite and we should all have hope in His forgiveness, for none of us sinners will earn entry into Paradise on merit alone, yet the warning of Allah's Messenger ﷺ should ring in our ears. Allah is not to be trifled with. When He has commanded us to behave a certain way and carry out particular actions, we *must* do as commanded. To ignore Him on the pretext that He will forgive us despite our worshipping our own whims and desires over Him is sheer stupidity.

Do not fear death but prepare to meet it. Death will be tasted by each of us, but we will only ever taste it once. The life of the Hereafter is forever and our ultimate goal must thus be to please Allah, so we may be granted the ecstasy of His Divine Company. Sayyidunā Abū Hurayrah رضي الله عنه narrated:

قَالَ رَسُولُ اللهِ صَلَّى اللهُ عَلَيْهِ وَسَلَّمَ أَتُضَامُونَ فِي رُؤْيَةِ الْقَمَرِ لَيْلَةَ الْبَدْرِ وَتُضَامُّونَ فِي رُؤْيَةِ الشَّمْسِ؟ قَالُوا لاَ. قَالَ فَإِنَّكُمْ سَتَرَوْنَ رَبَّكُمْ كَمَا تَرَوْنَ الْقَمَرَ لَيْلَةَ الْبَدْرِ لاَ تُضَامُّونَ فِي رُؤْيَتِهِ.

"Allah's Messenger ﷺ said, 'Do you struggle to see the Moon on a night when it is full? Do you struggle to see the Sun?' They said, 'No.' He said, 'Indeed you shall see your Lord as you see the Moon on a night when it is full. You will not struggle to see Him.'"[263]

May Allah grant us all this greatest of boons. *Āmīn*!

---

[262] *Sunan Ibn Mājah*, 4260.
[263] *Jāmi' al-Tirmidhī*, 2554.

5 | A FINAL WORD

The collection of hadiths that you have just read is but a drop in the ocean of scholarship that the great scholars of Islam have left us with. There are hundreds of books by far greater men and women than the compilers of this book that lay out in meticulous detail the qualities, characteristics, attributes, and duties of true *unūthah*, and we recommend that these are also studied and implemented. This book is a primer on the subject, aimed at a modernised, Western audience, and not to be taken as the sole manual to achieving perfect womanhood.

Modern society in the West has become a cesspit of decadence, disbelief, and immorality. As the wheels of time turn, the resoluteness of our wills to fight these evils is slowly being ground away. Generations come and go, each one weaker than the last, each one a step further off the beaten path to guidance and salvation. It often takes three generations before a people become wholly assimilated by the majority culture which surrounds them. This book has been written as the third generation of a large-scale Muslim presence grows to adulthood in the West, in the hope that we can correct our courses and return to the path. Perhaps we can bring those lost in the guideless wilds along with us.

The Sunnah of the Prophet ﷺ is universal. It spans both space and time, bridges ethnic and cultural divides, and provides us with a perfect example of how to live our lives in the world and for the Hereafter, through peace and war, in both safe and hostile environments. The sunnah of his Ṣaḥābah ﷽ is derived from their close proximity to him. If a narration is not attributed to the Prophet ﷺ but to his Ṣaḥābī ﷽, it does not mean that this was not the practice of the Prophet ﷺ. The

Ṣaḥābah ﷺ would not add anything to the religion of Islam beyond what they saw or heard from the Prophet ﷺ himself, and thus we can learn from their lives and their actions to obtain similar benefits. For this reason, it is also recommended that those who wish to study *unūthah* further should read the lives and biographies of the Ṣaḥābiyāt ﷺ. You will find no finer examples of true women than those chosen to be in the presence of Allah's Messenger ﷺ. Read about them, study them, and strive to be like them. Love what they loved, hate what they hated, and become better Muslimahs.

This book was primarily aimed at a female audience, though it is hoped that male readers will have also benefited from reading a primer on what makes the perfect woman, just as female readers hopefully benefitted from the companion collection, *40 Hadith on Masculinity: How to be a Good Man.*

If there were any mistakes in the body of the text, the translations of the Arabic, or elsewhere, then these are entirely the fault of the compilers of the text and we seek Allah's Protection, Forgiveness, and Mercy for our shortcomings. The Sunnah of the Prophet ﷺ is pure and without fault, whereas we, as poor excuses for his followers, are prone to mistakes and misunderstanding.

The zeitgeist of the modern-day Muslims in the West is one of self-deprecation and an acute awareness that we are not who and where we are supposed to be. Although this idea has some merit, it should not be viewed with the pessimism that many see it with; rather, we should study our social ills and correct them, striving to reach the heights of those pious predecessors who have gone before. Every generation of Muslims that followed the Prophetic Era lamented how far they had fallen, and every generation strived and struggled to be better Muslims. Our generation is no different.

The night is dark and the stars that guide us seem so far away...Yet their light still reaches us and, if we strain our eyes, we can still see the path to the luminous palaces of Paradise, hidden away just over the next horizon. Follow the path, follow the Sunnah, and you will soon reach the gates of salvation. Take heart, for your time in the Sun will come *in shā Allāh.*

سُبْحَانَكَ اللَّهُمَّ وَبِحَمْدِكَ، أَشْهَدُ أَنْ لاَ إِلَـهَ إِلاَّ أَنْتَ، أَسْتَغْفِرُكَ، وَأَتُوْبُ إِلَيْكَ.

Glory to You, O Allah, and praise be to You. I bear witness that there is none worthy of worship except You, I seek Your Forgiveness, and to You do I repent.[264]

[264] *Jāmiʿ al-Tirmidhī*, 3433.

www.ingramcontent.com/pod-product-compliance
Lightning Source LLC
Chambersburg PA
CBHW061150170426
43209CB00044B/1989/J
* 9 7 8 1 7 3 4 9 2 0 8 4 0 *